Connecting the Covenants

Connecting the Covenants

Judaism and the Search for Christian Identity in Eighteenth-Century England

DAVID B. RUDERMAN

PENN

University of Pennsylvania Press

Philadelphia

Printed in the United States of America on acid-free paper

10   9   8   7   6   5   4   3   2   1

Published by
University of Pennsylvania Press
Philadelphia, Pennsylvania 19104-4112

Library of Congress Cataloging-in-Publication Data

Ruderman, David B.
    Connecting the covenants : Judaism and the search for Christian identity in eighteenth-century England / David B. Ruderman.
        p. cm. — (Jewish culture and contexts)
    Includes bibliographical references and index.
    ISBN-13: 978-0-8122-4016-0 (hardcover : alk. paper)
    ISBN-10: 0-8122-4016-2 (hardcover : alk. paper)
    1. Judaism—Relations—Christianity—History—18th century. 2. Christianity and other religions—Judaism—History—18th century. 3. Marcus, Moses, b. 1701. 4. Christian converts from Judaism—England—Biography. 5. Judaism (Christian theology)—History of doctrines. 6. Hebraists, Christian—England—History—18th century. 7. Church of England—England—Clergy—History—18th century. 8. Jewish learning and scholarship—England—History—18th century. I. Title. II. Series.

BM535.R74 2007
261.2´6094209033—dc22

                                                                    2006102744

For Samuel Sklar,
physician and Hebrew humanist

Contents

viii   Contents

Introduction

The subject of this book lies at the interstices of Jewish and Christian history during the first decades of the eighteenth century. I attempt to reconstruct a fascinating moment in the reevaluation of post-biblical Judaism by a circle of Christian writers, many of them clerics, living primarily in England. Historians of Christianity have treated this subject only tangentially and cursorily while it has generally been ignored or passed over in silence by those who study Jewish history. As a historian whose primary interest is Jewish culture, I hope to recover its significance for Jewish as well as for Christian history.

The history of Jewish civilization in this era has been told and retold around certain prominent themes, often as discrete trajectories disconnected from each other. Recent scholarship has underscored the prolonged sense of crisis within the Jewish community precipitated by the messianic movement of Shabbetai Ẓevi in the late seventeenth century and the heresies that emerged in its wake throughout the eighteenth century,[1] as well as the shock waves generated by Benedict Spinoza's assault on Judaism and Christianity within the community of former *conversos* in Amsterdam and beyond.[2] Some have pointed to a perceived diminution of interest in Jewish culture and literature among Christian scholars by the beginning of the eighteenth century, which was replaced by a more critical and hostile posture toward Judaism.[3] Still others have focused on the concentration of large numbers of Jews living in Poland-Lithuania[4] and in the Ottoman Empire[5] and their relative isolation from cultural developments within western European civilization as a whole.

Most recently, several Jewish historians have underscored the importance of the cultural aspirations of a small group of Jewish intellectuals primarily living in central Europe at the beginning of the eighteenth century, even labeling them early *maskilim*.[6] In using this term to distinguish them from advocates of the later political and pedagogic movement known as the Haskalah appearing at the end of the century, they hope to locate the actual origins of the Jewish enlightenment in western and eastern Europe. Rather than clarifying this loosely knit group's relationship to later trends of the Enlightenment, they have primarily reinforced, to my mind, the sense of cultural ambiguity this murky period presents to Jewish historians and the need to see it more clearly in its own terms rather than as a mere prelude to later more definable cultural movements.

The subject of this book is quite different from all of these intellectual agendas. I wish to understand more clearly the preoccupation of certain Christian thinkers with Judaism as a critical religious and cultural factor and the ramifications of this preoccupation for both the history of Judaism and Christianity and their ongoing relations. Their discourses about Judaism took place in England and in English for the most part, although similar discussions can be located in Holland and elsewhere on the Continent in the first half of the eighteenth century. To a great extent, they represented a direct continuation of discussions of Judaism that had taken place among several prominent seventeenth-century scholars, although, as I shall argue, their more forceful emphasis and the language and context in which they emerged were different. In a manner not unlike that of the previous century, these extended conversations in which Judaism, its ancient history, and its classic texts played so central a role rarely involved Jewish interlocutors. When Christian thinkers required the expertise of Jewish languages and literature, they sometimes consulted former Jews or relied increasingly on a growing number of Christian scholars who had superficially or even thoroughly mastered Jewish texts. Jews accordingly remained on the margins of this activity, although they were never totally ignored by Christian contemporaries or totally oblivious to the discussions and the numerous publications about their own history and cultural legacy that featured so prominently within the larger public discourse of their society. Paradoxically, Christians often preferred to engage with Jewish ideas and texts rather than with actual Jews themselves.

My focus is on two separate stories that ultimately are interconnected. The first is about a colorful character known as Moses Marcus, a prominent young Jewish man who was baptized in the Anglican Church on New Year's Day, 1723. Marcus was also known by the Hebrew name of Moses ben Mordechai Hamburger and was the son of highly affluent parents and the grandson of the famous autobiographical author Glikl of Hameln.[7] His high profile immediately caught my attention among the biographies of similar converts of his era. Marcus was surely no ordinary candidate for church membership and undoubtedly represented a prize of some consequence to the missionaries who had succeeded in convincing him to repudiate his family's legacy. Marcus subsequently published a justification of his conversion and a strong vindication of his newly discovered faith in a small English book published in London in 1724. It was later enlarged and edited in a Dutch translation and published in Holland.[8]

Reading Marcus's book from cover to cover convinced me that this modest undertaking constituted more than a conventional narrative of a convert's dismissal of his ancestral faith and an emotional embrace of Christianity. It represented, to my knowledge, the first contemporary critical response to a much weightier volume composed by David Nieto, the dominant Jewish intellectual of London in the early eighteenth century and the rabbi of the Bevis Marks synagogue. Nieto had written an extensive and learned defense of the rabbis and the oral law in a work called *Ha-Kuzari ha-Sheni, Hu Mateh Dan,* which was published in London in 1714. I had previously studied Nieto and his famous work for an earlier book of mine wherein I suggested how Nieto had absorbed much of the theological and scientific ambiance of his immediate surroundings and used this knowledge in defense of the Jewish tradition.[9] That Marcus had dared to challenge directly this vaunted spokesman of traditional Judaism suggested a greater significance to Marcus's work than I had initially surmised.

Was the apparent disagreement between a famous Sephardic rabbi and a youthful neophyte from London recently educated in the Ashkenazic yeshivah of Hamburg ultimately part of a larger story worth telling? Nieto's spirited justification of the rabbis and the sanctity of the oral law has usually been linked to a larger rabbinic defense of traditional Judaism and its leadership that emerged in the late seventeenth century and continued throughout the eighteenth. As I have mentioned, rabbinic authority was thought to be in "crisis" because of the well-publicized assaults on its sanctity and legitimacy from such renegades as Uriel da Costa and Benedict Spinoza, because of the growing indifference to religious norms and practices on the part of a larger community of *conversos* in Amsterdam, Hamburg, and London, and because of the radical Sabbateans who had renounced the rabbinic establishment and its control over Jewish life in the name of their reputed messianic redeemer.[10]

Marcus's critique of Nieto's work, however, bears none of the markings of Spinozism, crypto-Judaism, or Sabbateanism; it is framed in an entirely different context. On the surface, it appears to be nothing more than a conventional Christian rejection of rabbinic Judaism, offering the rival claim that the true biblical religion sprouted from Christian soil, as reflected in the teachings of the New Testament and the church fathers, and not from that of the Pharisees and the rabbis and their allegedly stringent legal interpretations. But Marcus's essay represents more than the standard trope of Christian polemics against rabbinic Judaism. It offers, I believe, a window into a more complex and fascinating moment in the history of the two faiths, their relations with each other, and the role that theological discussion, informed especially by the knowledge of ancient religious history and texts, played in the public political, social, and cultural spheres of English society in the early decades of the eighteenth century. In using Marcus as my entry point, I think I have located a rich subject of a Jew who became a Christian, inhabited the liminal space of a convert betwixt and between the two faith communities, and attempted to build a solid reputation and achieve some modicum of material success in Christian high society as a kind of expert on Judaism and Hebraic learning. Most importantly, Marcus referred by name to many of his numerous associates and contacts, some of whom represented the actual religious and cultural elites of London's society. In identifying his network of social and professional connections, some superficial and some more meaningful, in examining his connections' own writings on Judaism and Christianity, and in exploring the points of agreement that connect them and the sharp disagreement that separates them, I hope to reconstruct a more significant conversation about Judaism and Christianity, their intertwined histories, and the contemporary strivings of Christians for relevance in a changing cultural and social world.

Marcus's modest successes in a world of the elite clerical establishment in London were followed by conspicuous failures, both intellectual and material. His hopes to be accepted by the Christian intellectual community as a prominent expert in Judaism were ultimately dashed due to his own social and scholarly limitations and by the unimaginative ways in which he presented his former ancestral faith to his new co-religionists. The Christian theologians with whom he sought to ingratiate himself had a wider and more penetrating vision of post-biblical Judaism than he could ever have perceived. His mere textual competency in both biblical and rabbinic studies never allowed him to grasp fully what his Christian associates were ultimately gleaning from their rich exposure to Jewish texts. He remained torn and divided between the faith of his parents and that of his newly adopted church, never capable of discovering the means to reconcile the two. To the extent that his later life is known, he appears to have died a broken and defeated man; the severe decline of his economic status precisely mirrored his diminishing value to Christian scholars as a so-called expert on Judaism. While he attempted to defend the integrity of biblical Judaism and Jews in his writings, he could not free himself simultaneously from criticizing rabbinic Judaism, its exegesis, its praxis, its oral law, and especially its claims to speak the divine truth independent of the rival claims of Christianity. In the final analysis, Marcus was outstripped and superseded by the very same coterie of Christian intellectuals he assumed would become his grateful pupils in mastering Judaism.

My second story emerges against the background of Marcus's professional decline and ultimate failure as a cultural mediator between Judaism and Christianity. As a narrow textual specialist, Marcus was hardly a creative thinker capable of understanding more profoundly how the two religious traditions actually might cohere and speak meaningfully to each other. The latter task was assumed by a group of Christian theologians, some of whom Marcus had even personally encountered. Their aspirations in studying Judaism surely transcended Marcus's competency and vision. They sought ambitiously to master the entire corpus of rabbinic Judaism, to imbibe the exegetical methodology of the rabbis, to appreciate the historical context of post-biblical Judaism for understanding the birth of Christianity, and even to acknowledge the spiritual essence of the religion the rabbis had shaped. Responding creatively to the acute challenges then offered by historicism, philology, and antiquarian scholarship, forcing themselves to reassess and revalidate the present in terms of an increasingly confusing and slippery past, they found the study of rabbinic Judaism a critical resource in fortifying their own Christian identities.

In following Marcus's path from the yeshivah world of Hamburg to an elite society of English theologians and church leaders in London, but then turning from him to the larger concerns of this latter group, I think I have found a novel way of illuminating a highly significant but relatively neglected chapter in the long and complex history of the Jewish-Christian encounter. Although the initial protagonist of my story is a Jew who opted out of Judaism, the story I hope to relate clearly transcends his personal odyssey and his confused identity between Judaism and Christianity. Ultimately, the most important story of this book is the second one: the creative uses of Judaism by Christian writers who dramatically surpassed this mediating figure in their more sustained effort to reconcile the two faiths in a moment of crisis for both.

At the beginning of the eighteenth century, Jewish and Christian religious leaders faced a common predicament: the need to justify their contemporary faiths in the light of new scholarly discoveries of philologists and historians that not only clouded their respective origins but also obfuscated and confused the seemingly self-evident connections between the biblical foundation of their religions and their later transformations into Judaism and Christianity. As Justin Champion has so eloquently argued, politicians, clerics, and laity alike in this era assumed that cultural authority was based on scholarly discourse. This meant, in the context of the protracted skirmishes among high and low clergy, Latitudinarians, Socinians, and deists, that biblical and patristic scholarship along with knowledge of ancient history and philology were all crucial instruments for the ideological justification of clerical as well as civil authority. This was a significant moment in the history of ideas, where historical scholarship had assumed so formidable a role in shaping public opinion. It was also a critical period in the study of religion since it was increasingly assumed that religions also had a history, humanly conceived and humanly generated, and that they were only understandable when they defined themselves in historical terms. The ultimate impact of this explosion of new scholarly studies and new textual editions, as well as the discovery of new sources, both real and contrived, was to create an uncertainty about origins that ultimately led to a lack of clarity and indeterminacy about the present. The new historical criticism ultimately muddied the waters of the past. The bedrock of Christianity, the fulfillment of the Old Testament in the New, as well as the previously impervious boundaries between Judaism and Christianity, between canonical and apocryphal, and between orthodox and heretical had all been called into question. Historical scholarship could rethink all previous assumptions, rendering precarious what Champion called "the cultural keystone of order."[11]

It is in the context of the cultural crisis so well interpreted by Champion that I wish to place this work. A renewed interest in Judaism emerged in these clerical circles at the same time that they were entangled in and confounded by ideological conflicts fueled by the bewildering advances of historical and philological scholarship. It was inevitable that the study of ancient Christian origins would lead ultimately to a rethinking of Jewish origins as well, and that the disdain and indifference that had characterized centuries of Christian attitudes toward postbiblical Judaism were in need of reevaluation. In feverishly scouring the past to locate and appropriate new resources for understanding what the "primitive church" actually was, Christian scholars eventually were obliged to confront the literature and culture of the rabbis as well. In the end, Moses Marcus never rose to the challenge of "connecting the covenants" between the Old and the New Testaments, on the one hand, and between the written and oral law, on the other, that is, of connecting the two strands of his own religious identity. That was left to the Christian elite community he had hoped to serve, who responded more profoundly and creatively to this new challenge.

The book opens with a consideration of a strong disagreement in print that emerged several years before Marcus published his initial work. There is no evidence that the two protagonists actually knew each other or were even aware of each other's writing, even though both documents were published in London within a span of two years. Nevertheless, when one reads their publications side by side, one might surmise that had the two sat in the same room together, they would have certainly engaged in heated debate. I refer to the famous English history of ancient Judaism and early Christianity by Humphrey Prideaux, the Christian cleric and scholar, entitled appropriately *The Old and New Testament Connected,* whose first volume appeared in London in 1716, and David Nieto's aforementioned defense of rabbinic Judaism published in Hebrew and Spanish in the same city in 1714. While legitimating the "connections" between Hebraic Scripture and early Christianity, Prideaux simultaneously negated the claims of the rabbis that their Judaism truly reflected the biblical faith. On the contrary, Prideaux claimed, the rabbinic legacy was a human-made fabrication bearing little resemblance to its biblical counterpart and representing a distortion of its guiding principles, which were fully represented, in contrast, by Anglican Christianity.

Nieto's elegant defense of rabbinic Judaism rested on the assumption that such accusations, insinuating that the rabbis had created a new law of their own making, were utterly false. On the contrary, he argued, the divine law was impenetrable without the clarifications and specifications of the rabbinic exegetes. The conflicting postures of these two authors' publications, addressed to different audiences and in different languages, surely set the stage for the direct challenge posed to Nieto by Moses Marcus in his own conversionary tract written a few years later. In the context of the well-publicized presentations of the rabbi and the Christian scholar, Moses Marcus's own arguments, mirroring those of Prideaux, make sense as an accurate reflection of contemporary Christian sentiment about rabbinic Judaism and as a justification of the publication of his book by his Christian sponsors in the first place.

Chapter 2 considers the circumstances that led Moses Marcus to embrace the Anglican Church. His early years first revolved around the complex experiences of his father, known as Marcus Moses, who rose to affluence and power in London, disagreed bitterly with the chief rabbi (Aaron Hart, also known as Uri Phoebus), was "excommunicated," and lived in long-term "exile" in India as a successful diamond merchant. I speculate on the circumstances of Moses Marcus's conversion both in Hamburg and in London; his special relationship with his learned Anglican mentor, David Wilkins, the house chaplain to the archbishop of Canterbury; and his growing ambivalence about living as a Christian while maintaining strong family and intellectual links with Jewish culture that he apparently could never fully disown. This ambivalence is especially prominent in his seemingly contradictory action of suing his own father in an attempt to retain the material support he had apparently relinquished through his conversion, while at the same time apparently reclaiming his former Jewish identity during the extended period of the court proceedings. That a Jewish family dispute could figure so prominently in the protracted proceedings of a civil court also suggests the well-publicized nature of this entire affair.

In Chapter 3, I continue to trace Moses Marcus's career as a convert, particularly his efforts to showcase his expertise on Jewish matters before Christian clergy who apparently valued this knowledge. Reconstructing this career is made feasible by the discovery of a begging letter he wrote to Lord Hans Sloane in the 1730s in which he specifically mentioned his manifold writings, both printed and in manuscript, and his long list of patrons, a virtual road map of the social and professional networks he created with church leaders, theologians, and writers. The letter, along with his other correspondence and writings on Judaism, allow us to construct a full-blown portrait of his rise to limited fame, albeit accompanied by professional instability and eventual economic failure. Marcus was ultimately a conflicted man who openly attacked the foundations of the oral law while, at the same time, functioning as a conduit, even as an advocate, for the fair and accurate presentation of Judaism to Christians. His conversion was accordingly never final or complete; his life and writing reveal how consistent and sincere he remained in his ambivalence, lingering between his former and his present faiths.

Whatever name Marcus attained in the elite world of Christian clerics came through the brief pamphlet he penned defending the integrity of Dr. Daniel Waterland, the foremost orthodox Anglican theologian of his day, against his learned and unconventional critic Conyers Middleton. The remainder of the chapter looks closely at Marcus's relationship to Waterland and to his associate Zachary Pearce, contextualizing his modest publication in defense of biblical circumcision within the larger struggle between the orthodox Anglican camp and its more radical critics.

Chapter 4 addresses Marcus's more ambitious project of translating from Latin into English the work of the German biblical scholar Johann Gottlob Carpzov. In this work, Marcus again identified himself with the traditionalist camp, attacking a recent controversial book by William Whiston, who was a Newtonian scientist, a historian, and a theologian. Whiston's attempt to locate a literal "scientific" correlation between the prophecies of the Old Testament and references in the New had obliged him to conclude that the traditional Masoretic Hebrew text of the Bible had been corrupted by the Jews. This position was personally repugnant to Marcus and subsequently he came to defend the integrity of the Hebrew Bible through his translation and annotation of Carpzov's weighty critique.

Marcus's effort in presenting Carpzov to an English-reading audience connected him personally to a much larger controversy surrounding Whiston's intellectual project. This was precipitated by an even more caustic critique of Whiston by the well-known free thinker Anthony Collins. In comparing Collins's critique of Whiston with that of Carpzov and Marcus, one can easily detect how the terms of the debate concerning how one reads the New Testament in relationship to the Old were radically changing. Collins vigorously attacked Whiston's "Newtonian" solution of connecting the Old and the New Testaments and his emphatic claim that a literal correspondence between the two testaments was possible. Collins insisted that the only way to read the New Testament was in a figurative, metaphorical manner, most often associated with that of Jewish exegetes. He further argued that the most efficacious way to understand the appropriate context, language, and style of the New Testament was through a solid grounding in rabbinic hermeneutics. This he had learned from reading the journal of the Huguenot author and editor Michel de la Roche and his careful summary of the methods of the Dutch scholar William Surenhusius, the editor and translator of the recent Latin edition of the Mishnah with its medieval commentaries. Most interpreters of Collins's demolition of Whiston's argument present him as insincere and disingenuous. How ironic it must have appeared that only the rabbis might save the Christians from the seemingly impossible bind of not comprehending properly their sacred Scripture! In offering to save Christianity through the agency of rabbinic exegesis, Collins was cynically destroying the very foundation of the traditional Christian faith.

Collins's clever rebuttal of Whiston, including his creative use of La Roche and through him, Surenhusius, require a fresh reading along with some of the numerous responses that Collins himself provoked among Christian intellectuals. This is the subject of Chapter 5. Should the approach of Surenhusius in utilizing the rabbis to understand Christianity be dismissed out of hand as the musings of an eccentric scholar, or did he in fact have an impact and a following in England itself? Whether or not Collins was sincere in what he wrote about Surenhusius, the latter was indeed taken seriously by several of his contemporaries who increasingly were becoming convinced that the rabbinic tradition was useful in explicating Christianity. A Christian scholar could only ignore this body of literature at the risk of inadequately understanding the foundations of his own faith.

The primary exponent of the methods of Surenhusius in England was the well known defender of modern wisdom over that of the ancients, William Wotton. His Hebraic studies and in particular his justification of the use of the Mishnah for understanding ancient Christianity are the subject of Chapter 6. Not only did Wotton assert his commitment to rabbinic learning as a Christian in a long essay, but he actually translated several parts of the Mishnah into English with extensive commentary. In this he was aided and supported by Simon Ockley, the well-known Cambridge professor of Islamic history who wrote a favorable endorsement of Wotton's project that was printed in the work itself. Another of his collaborators was David Wilkins, the chaplain of William Wake, the archbishop of Canterbury, and coincidently the primary mentor of Moses

Marcus, whom Wilkins had guided to the baptismal font of the Anglican Church in the first place. But despite the indirect connection between Marcus and Wotton through Wilkins, the gulf separating the convert from this learned Christian exegete and his friends is strikingly apparent. Wotton, following Surenhusius and his disciples, understood the rabbis in a manner notably dissimilar from that of Marcus.

In the conclusion, I point out how this reconstruction of Marcus's life and writing and his mediating role among Jews and Christian theologians provides an opening to a novel world of Christian engagement with Judaism in the early eighteenth century, a world that Marcus himself never fully entered or comprehended. Marcus, like most Christians in early modern Europe, still remained locked in the theological language of the traditional Jewish-Christian debate, attempting to validate his newly adopted religious identity by invalidating the other, specifically the exposition of David Nieto to which he offered his counterargument. Yet against the backdrop of a new explosion in historical scholarship and textual philology, upsetting and complicating conventional assessments of the Christian past, a new approach was emerging, one unimagined and unanticipated by Moses Marcus or Humphrey Prideaux or even David Nieto himself. Christians such as William Surenhusius and William Wotton had become acutely aware of the critical importance of rabbinic culture for penetrating the obscure origins of Christianity. Overcoming long-felt inhibitions about seriously engaging with Judaism and its normative texts, while drawing inspiration from a small circle of gifted researchers of the seventeenth century who had preceded them, they came to appreciate more than ever a culture and literature from which the overwhelming majority of Christians had distanced themselves. What was at stake for them was more than merely satisfying their scholarly and antiquarian interests. They were convinced they were retrieving a vital part of themselves in this quest to unearth the Jewish past. And their bold declarations vindicating their carefully conceived positions, written increasingly in English, were noticed and received favorably by a wider community of theologians, church leaders, and educated laypersons than ever before. In their bewildering world of competing theological and political claims emanating from a fractured Christian community at war with itself, one might perhaps discern in such modest efforts of self-discovery a more tolerant, nuanced, and appreciative attitude toward Judaism as a cultural factor, if not toward actual Jews themselves.

Chapter 1

Covenants Connected and Unconnected: David Nieto and His Anglican Adversaries, Humphrey Prideaux and Moses Marcus

When David Nieto (1654–1728) arrived in London from his native Livorno in Italy at the beginning of the eighteenth century to assume the post of *ḥakham* of the Spanish and Portuguese Synagogue, he had presumably prepared well for the task. Educated as a physician at Padua, armed with a wide-ranging education in traditional Jewish sources, sufficiently familiar with the elite Christian world based on personal contact with Christian intellectuals, and with a reading knowledge in several languages including Latin, he easily towered over other Jewish leaders in England and was taken seriously by Jews and Christians alike both in England and on the Continent. A false accusation that he had Spinozist leanings, based on a single utterance misconstrued in one of his sermons, could not ultimately damage his high reputation within his community. The publication of several of his books, especially his magnum opus, *Ha-Kuzari ha-Sheni, Hu Mateh Dan,* published in 1714 in two simultaneous editions in Hebrew and Spanish, represented a kind of apex of his distinguished career and assured him a reputation as a leading spokesman of traditional Judaism far beyond the confines of London.[1]

Nieto's vigorous defense of rabbinic law and praxis, in which he presented his own articulation of Judaism as a kind of updating and refinement of the classic work of the medieval thinker Yehudah ha-Levi, has generally been contextualized as a direct response to the apathy and self-doubt of his primary constituency in London, a congregation of Sephardic Jews, former *conversos,* who needed to be reminded of the cogency and relevance of traditional Judaism in a culture where secularization and acculturation were rampant. As in the case of ha-Levi, Nieto singled out the "Karaites," the traditional medieval critics of rabbinical Judaism as the primary target of his polemic against those who had previously sought to undermine the basic premises of traditional Judaism, but it is not clear at all whether he had in mind only them along with their descendents still present in his own generation.[2] He also singled out a gathering "of wise men in their own eyes"[3] who did not acknowledge the Torah of their rabbis, an equally ambiguous label. Because he failed to specify a particular address for his remarks, scholars have generally assumed that he meant simply all those Jews of his generation who had challenged rabbinic authority at its core, that is, Jewish enthusiasts driven by either messianic zeal or by rationalistic proclivities to question the very validity of the rabbinic construction of Judaism. Nieto later penned a short diatribe against the Sabbatean infidel Nehemiah Ḥayon,[4] and he was intimately familiar with the heresies associated with Spinoza's name that had personally tarnished his good reputation at the beginning of his tenure in London.[5] It stood to reason that these general enemies of the rabbinic establishment were the real audience he wanted to address, and since he published his work in Hebrew accompanied by a Spanish translation, he was speaking simultaneously to a Hebraicly literate audience of Jews and possibly some Christians, as well as a larger community of highly assimilated Sephardim whose primary language was Spanish or Portuguese.

It has been commonly assumed that Nieto knew little English, at least during his initial years in England, nor did he preach in that language. Over the course of the several decades of his English career, however, he seems to have read considerably in the theological and scientific writing of his immediate surroundings, perhaps initially in Latin alone, but ultimately in English as well. If I am correct in my earlier reconstruction of his thinking, that he had familiarized himself with some of the Christian theology of his day and appropriated it in constructing his own exposition of Judaism, then we might assume that he was generally well read and up-to-date, especially about matters that meant the most to him, such as the new scientific cosmologies of Newton and his contemporaries and their creative application in demonstrating the truth of religious faith. Indeed, Nieto's formulation of Jewish faith along the lines of the famous Boyle lectures of Samuel Clarke, demonstrating the veracity of Judaism in the light of the new scientific discoveries, is so close to Clarke's own words that it strongly suggests that he had heard or read Clarke directly.[6]

In returning again to the specific context of English Christianity for a full understanding of Nieto's work, I would like to suggest an alternative way to read his well-crafted arguments on behalf of traditional Judaism and also to propose how they might have been received by those Anglican theologians who were in a position to notice his work in the first place. Admittedly, my evidence is quite slim in arguing for any broad reception of his book at all among England's Christian intellectual community. Nevertheless, Nieto was never an isolated figure; he definitely had his Christian associates in London and on the Continent.[7] Most importantly, the arguments he made were especially relevant to them in that they seemed to refute directly some common Christian perceptions of rabbinic

Judaism. And in the case of Moses Marcus, a recent convert to Anglicanism whose work was surely supported by clerics of high authority within the church, Nieto's arguments did in fact elicit a direct refutation.

In dialogical form, Nieto proceeded to argue vigorously that the oral interpretations of the rabbis were divinely inspired and were indispensable for a proper understanding of the Hebrew Bible. The rabbis had no reason to concoct rulings unrelated to the divine law; they were fully committed to the sanctity of the text they were interpreting; and thus what they derived was a faithful rendering of its original meaning. Judah the Prince merely edited the Mishnah based on generations of oral interpretations that he had collected. The rabbis, Nieto further contended, were humble and God-fearing and had no desire to use their rulings to dominate their constituency. When they argued with each other, their arguments never involved first principles but only practical considerations. Ultimately, an oral tradition was committed to writing as it was in danger of being forgotten. Its functionality is self-evident; for without it, the Bible remains a closed book and a generalized law code without practical application.[8]

Nieto also maintained that the Bible itself sanctioned oral interpretation, citing especially the critical passages in Deut. 17:8–13: "If a case is too baffling for you to decide, be it a controversy over homicide, civil law, or assault—matters of disputes in your courts—you should promptly repair to the place which the Lord your God will have chosen, and appear before the levitical priests, or the magistrate in charge at the time, and present your problem. When they have announced to you the verdict in the case, you shall carry out the verdict that is announced to you from that place that the Lord chose, observing scrupulously all their instructions to you." The mandate to turn to authorities in each generation was thus realized by rabbinic judges who never imagined they were enlarging or transforming the original intention of the divine will to create another law unrelated to the original. Because they were scrupulously honest, they clearly indicated when a ruling of theirs was not biblically grounded and when it was. In sum, the oral law of Judaism was always coterminous with the written, being given at Sinai, and the existence of the oral was always presupposed in the written.[9]

Nieto's arguments relied heavily on those of earlier defenders of the oral tradition such as Moses Maimonides and, of course, ha-Levi. His most original contribution was his discussion of the enduring value of rabbinic sapience over the regnant scientific theories of his day, which were speculative and capable at any time of being overturned. The rest of the argument advocating the unbroken chain of authority between the biblical text and its rabbinic interpretation rested firmly on his earlier sources. The simplicity of the dialogical argument and the elegance and the accessibility of the printed editions were especially effective. It was a message comprehensible enough to be grasped by a young student, a kind of catechism to provide a rationale and an endorsement of the process of rabbinic education the student was about to undertake.

Humphrey Prideaux (1648–1724), the dean of Norwich, was a contemporary of Nieto and published his major works as a Christian scholar of Judaism and Islam at about the same time Nieto's publications had begun to appear. Prideaux was especially well known for his *Life of Mahomet,* which appeared in 1697. Prideaux's Arabic sources were entirely based on printed editions and he relied heavily on the previous work of Edward Pococke (1604–91). Nevertheless, the work was popular as a highly subjective polemic against Islamic claims to religious truth. Prideaux was also an accomplished Hebrew scholar, having published a Latin translation and commentary of a section of Maimonides's law code entitled *De jure pauperis et peregrini* as early as 1679. His most significant work, however, was his *The Old and New Testament Connected in the History of the Jews and Neighboring Nations from the Declension of the Kingdoms of Israel and Judah to the Time of Christ,* which was first published in two volumes between 1716 and 1718, only a few years after Nieto's publication. The work was republished several times and in several languages and served as the basis of a number of later works of ancient religious history. Prideaux treated the history of the Jews from 747 B.C. to 292 B.C. in the first volume, and then to A.D. 33 in the second. Here too he relied heavily on an earlier work by James Usher (1581–1656), but, as in the case of his life of Muhammad, he wrote elegantly and simply, making his history one of the most popular and accessible to a wide readership well into the nineteenth century.[10]

That Prideaux failed to notice Nieto's book seems somewhat surprising given his impressive citations of other Hebrew books and authors, some of them of relatively recent date. They include such works as *Sefer Yuḥasim, Seder Olam, Shalshelet ha-Kabbalah* by Gedaliah ibn Yaḥya, *Ẓemaḥ David* by David Gans, the writings of Isaac Abravanel, Azariah de' Rossi, Moses Naḥmanides, David Kimḥi, Abraham Saba, and Levi ben Gershon, the Zohar, and more. His Hebraic erudition was matched by his attention to the Babylonian and Persian backgrounds of his story and by his use of the best of recent Christian scholars, such as Johannes Buxtorf, John Selden, Thomas Hyde, Stephanus Morinus, and more.[11]

Ostensibly a history, the title of his work conveys his primary concern, which becomes especially prominent at the point at which the narrative takes up the story of Ezra and subsequent Jewish history. Prideaux's initial description of the oral law seems innocuous enough: "For the Law they say was given by Moses, but it was revived and restored by Ezra after it had been in a Manner extinguished and lost in the Babylonian captivity. In Ezra's time, they gave birth to what the Jews now call their Oral Law.

For they own a twofold Law, the first the Written Law, which is recorded in the Holy Scriptures, and the second, the Oral Law, which they have only by the Tradition of their Elders. And both these, they say, were given them by Moses from Mount Sinai."[12] Prideaux also reports that the Jews feel more bound by the oral than the written law because they contend that the latter is "obscure, scanty, and defective, and could be no perfect Rule to them without the Oral Law."[13]

To this point, Prideaux had seemingly summarized the Jewish position, a description with which Nieto himself would not have taken issue. But Prideaux could no longer restrain his anger regarding this Jewish invention: "And therefore they do in a Manner lay aside the former to make room for the latter, and resolve their whole Religion into their Traditions, in the same manner as the Romanists [i.e., the Catholics] do theirs, having no further regard to the written Word of God, than as it agrees with their traditionary explications of it." Citing Mark 7:13—"They make the Word of God of none effect through their Traditions"—Prideaux had no doubt that the rabbis had introduced a new religion to replace the old, or as he put it, the written law became for them "the dead letter" while their traditions alone constituted the "soul." The verdict then was clear: "But all this is mere Fiction, spun out of the fertile Invention of the Talmudists, without the least Foundation either in Scripture, or in any authentic History of it." What Prideaux particularly understood was the evolutionary process the rabbis had put into motion, each generation adding its imaginative musings to the previous one, so that "these Traditions becoming as a Snowball, the further they rouled down from one Generation to another, the more they gathered, and the greater the Bulk of them grew."[14]

All of this disapproval of rabbinic distortion is balanced by an accurate description of the Mishnah and the Gemarah, the Babylonian and Palestinian Talmuds, and the positive contribution rabbinic texts have made in elucidating the New Testament, especially the Aramaic *targumim,* which "very much serve the Christian cause against the Jews by interpreting many of the Prophecies of the Messiah in the Old Testament in the same Manner as the Christians do."[15] But in the final analysis the rabbinic enterprise, is corrupting and inauthentic in setting up the Talmud as a replacement of the Bible, in the same manner that the Roman Catholic Church has substituted canon law for the biblical word. The rabbis accordingly can be labeled Jewish Catholics, presenting a falsification of and an inauthentic replica of the original biblical religion. Given the intensity with which Prideaux argued his case, Nieto's arguments, had they been seen by the Christian scholar, might have evoked a strong rebuttal on his part.

Some twenty years later the deist writer Thomas Morgan, in his popular work *The Moral Philosopher*, which was published in 1737, reiterated Prideaux's point, even citing him by name, thus capturing precisely the significance of this message for *The Old and New Testament Connected*. Morgan called the process Prideaux had described "a great Revolution in Religion" whereby the rabbis innovated by citing Moses "not in the original, proper, and literal sense of those Authors themselves, but in their own new, figurative, and allegorical sense, by which they could make them speak whatever they pleased." In Morgan's retelling, the rabbis were conflated not with Catholics but with kabbalists, and their snowball of interpretations could be understood as mystical and allegorical: "In and after the days of Ezra, the Jewish Cabbalists, under the Pretence of an oral Tradition from Moses, introduced a mystical sense of their original books, and under that Pretence put what construction they pleased upon the Law." Morgan also cited Prideaux in seeking a reason for this radical change:

> that the common People having then lost their original Language after their Captivity, were obliged to receive both the true Reading and Sense of their antient sacred books from their learned doctors the Masorites and Cabbalists: which gave these learned Gentlemen an opportunity to advance and propagate what Doctrines they pleased under the Authority of Moses and the Prophets; and because they could not pretend to support such new Doctrine from the original, proper, and literal sense of the text which they read and expounded; therefore they set up an oral Tradition to justify their arbitrary Interpretations as the Papists had done since.

Morgan had related succinctly the gist of Prideaux's reconstruction of rabbinic Judaism and had embellished it only by his conflation of other Jewish "Papists," that is, Masorites, who had supplied points to the biblical text, and kabbalists, who had inserted their mystical and figurative interpretations. Morgan's grasp of these matters surely typified a common sentiment shared by all kinds of Christians of his day. That his primary source for this insight was Prideaux's history is one small indication of the contemporary impact of this text.[16]

A decade after Nieto's book had been published and some eight years after that of Prideaux, a twenty-three-year-old convert to Christianity named Moses Marcus published a small book in London in 1724 entitled *The Principal Motives and Circumstances That Induced Moses Marcus to Leave the Jewish, and Embrace the Christian Faith*.[17] The work represents a personal account and justification of Marcus's decision to leave Judaism for Anglican Christianity. It represents a major source of Marcus's biography and will be examined more carefully as such in the next chapter. What is particularly relevant here is its obsession with the invalidity of the oral law, mirroring Prideaux's arguments, and its direct refutation of Nieto's defense.

Marcus's first direct reference to *Ha-Kuzari ha-Sheni, Hu Mateh Dan* follows a long discussion of the Talmud and rabbinic law toward the end of his book, in which he writes: "But what amazes me in the highest Degree, is a Book lately printed in London entitled Cuzeri by the Jewish hakham Rabbi David Netto, chiefly containing a Vindication of the Oral Law; but full of Absurdities and Superstitions, and wherein he asserts, that the chief Substance and Marrow of the Jewish Faith consists in the Oral Law. But the chief Substance of this Work is nothing but impertinent Parables, having nothing from Scripture, to prove that the Oral Law is the chief Foundation of the Jewish Religion."[18]

Marcus focuses directly on Nieto's most substantial discussion of the matter, his exegesis of Deuteronomy 17. He first brings Nieto's citation of Rashi on Deut. 17:11: "That if the Judge or the Body of the Sanhedrin should judge that thy right Hand is thy left, or thy left Hand is thy right; nevertheless, less thou shalt obey them." He then relates Nieto's use of a parable of a king who appointed a governor and commanded that his subjects obey him fully. The governor issued a proclamation prohibiting anyone from holding iron instruments. When a person was apprehended with a knife, he pleaded in his defense that knives had not been singled out, only the general category of iron instruments. This was of no avail and all knives were confiscated by the will of the governor. For Nieto, God's will could be carried out only by designating to his governors, that is, the rabbis, the appropriate license to interpret his will.[19]

Marcus objects to the lesson of the parable which he considers to be "without reason or foundation." At the same time, no one should follow blindly the will of judges over the precepts of the Almighty and condemn the innocent to death. The parable does not indicate to what extent the governor was actually God-fearing and a man of superior moral character. Marcus continues to rebut Nieto's further arguments about how the rabbis presumed to know the exact type of fruit to be used in the Sukkot ritual, claiming sarcastically that their opinion "was instituted by the Almighty on Mount Sinai." He concludes his long refutation of the core of Nieto's arguments by insisting that the oral law is arbitrarily based on human error and does not reflect the divine law.[20]

Marcus's direct refutation of Nieto represents the culmination of his constant barrage of arguments condemning the foundations of rabbinic authority through the oral law, pointing out the absurdities of talmudic passages and the contradictions the rabbis often make. He underscores the notions that rabbinic law is humanly constructed, not divinely conceived; that the rabbis cannot claim any legitimate chain of authority stemming from the prophets; that the Talmud insults Christians and induces messianic delusions like those of Shabbetai Ẓevi; and that the Talmud is of medieval origin, composed of stories even taken from the Muslim Koran. In contrast to the oral law, all of the Old Testament prophecies concerning the Messiah were fulfilled by Jesus. In sum, Marcus concludes: "Thus you plainly perceive your pernicious Superstitions and Delusions; your Contradictions and Prevarications; all of which leave no Room to doubt, but that the Christian faith is better grounded on the sacred Scripture than your traditional faith."[21]

Marcus's critique of the oral law differs from that of Prideaux in some obvious ways: it was written by an insider who personalized his disillusion with rabbinic Judaism and his inspiration to embrace the church; it took notice and commented directly on Nieto's volume, especially his major arguments interpreting Deuteronomy 17; and it revealed the innocent style of a young writer lacking the pretentious scholarship and heavy annotation of a seasoned researcher. But it still bears a resemblance to Prideaux's arguments. Both authors point out the flawed logic of insisting that human exegesis is divine law; they both appreciate, nevertheless, that certain aspects of rabbinic literature can be utilized to support Christian positions, especially the Aramaic *targumim*; and they both adopt a Protestant argument of equating rabbinic practice with that of the Catholic Church.

We will soon have occasion to explore further the particular circumstances that occasioned the writing of Marcus's treatise. What might be stated from the outset is that both Marcus's conversion and the publication of this relatively sophisticated critique of Judaism, including a fearless challenge to the most important Jewish intellectual in England, could not have taken place without the full weight of the Anglican authorities behind it. As we shall see, David Wilkins, Marcus's mentor who supervised his conversion and offered his own endorsement of Marcus in the book itself, held the important position of personal chaplain to the archbishop of Canterbury, William Wake. Marcus's composition was even dedicated to Wake directly. There is no doubt that the church officials supervising Marcus's conversion knew they were dealing with at least a minor celebrity, the first son of the wealthiest Jew in London, one educated in Judaism and in general culture, and one ready to embarrass his parents to win material support for himself and vindication for his newly adopted faith. It is inconceivable that Marcus produced his volume and its argument without their direct support and approval. In other words, the work had the markings of at least a semi-official publication of the Anglican Church. Considered together with the work of Prideaux, it most probably reflected the "party line," that is, an indirect acknowledgment that the church was aware of Nieto's spirited defense of rabbinic Judaism and that it sought to counter and demolish his primary arguments. It is hard to imagine how a young man in his early twenties could have undertaken such a task without such direct supervision. If indeed Marcus's book was an initiative of the Anglicans themselves, together with the work of Prideaux, it suggests the emergence of a public position, or, more precisely, the public reiteration of a traditional position regarding the oral law. At least two Christians, one an accomplished theologian and one a young neophyte, understood rabbinic Judaism well enough to undermine its theoretical foundations, as well as to challenge the arguments of its most able advocate.

Chapter 2

Moses Marcus's Conversion to Christianity

Moses Marcus, the author of the *Principal Motives,* was born in London in 1701, the first son of Mordechai Hamburger ben Moses Loeb of Altona and Freudchen bat Ḥayyim Hameln. Freudchen, his mother, was one of the twelve children of Ḥayyim and Glikl of Hameln; Glikl was the famous author of an autobiography who was still alive when Moses converted to Christianity in 1723. Moses' parents seem to have settled in London only a few years before his birth. His father, Mordechai, known in English sources as Marcus Moses, was himself the son of a distinguished and affluent rabbinical family. Marcus and Freudchen (Joy) were part of a migration of Jewish families from the area of Hamburg and Altona who discovered London to be hospitable, especially for its economic opportunities.[1]

Marcus Moses quickly rose to prominence in the diamond business of London along with several other Jewish businessmen, especially his close associate, Abraham Nathan. In fact, in the early years of the eighteenth century several Jews in London seem to have controlled a major share of the diamond and coral trade, and Moses was one of the most prominent in this group. Initially these merchants were content to buy Indian diamonds only after they had been shipped to London. Moses apparently ran his business from London alone at least until 1713. During these years his legal associate was Sir Richard Hoare, who represented him in several transactions as a number of letters indicate. In 1712 Moses was in Paris with a model of the famous Pitt diamond. Through his association with Pitt, he was introduced there to Pierre Dulivier, the governor of the Indian settlement of Pondicherry, who subsequently invited him to settle temporarily in this French colony.

In 1713, with the support of the French East India Company, Moses became the first Jew to travel to Pondicherry, apparently convinced by the French that he could break the English monopoly of diamond sales through mining in this rival Indian settlement. The effort seems to have failed, however, and by 1715, he had moved to the English settlement of Madras. In need of cash to make the move, Moses drew up a bill of exchange in India mentioning the names of his wife, Joy, and his son Moses

Marcus, and signing the document in English as Marcus Moses and in Hebrew as Mordechai Hamburger. Moses subsequently stayed in Madras until 1721, when he returned to London with considerable wealth, immediately prior to the time his son Moses Marcus announced his conversion to Christianity. Despite his huge resources, he was forced to return to India in 1728 after having fallen into bankruptcy. His return to India coincided unfortunately with the discovery of diamonds in Brazil and he continued to struggle with his declining business.[2]

The British Library owns a letter penned by Marcus Moses in 1731 to an I. Pyke and C. Laquier, offering a rare glimpse of his aggressive efforts to promote his business from afar. He wrote the following lines in less than elegant English to his prospective customers in London:

I hope this will find you in good Health and I am in the same, thank God. Now I be so good as my promise and send you by George Capt. Pitt a small box directed to you where you will find ten small bags of sand and stones where the Diamonds grow among, and written about every bag the names of the head places where they grow. There is abundance of small places more, where this is Mines, but all in the same manner and here goes by an enclosed account signed by all eminent miners that liveth in the mines and also testified by the principal diamond merchants of Madrasse. . . . I would beg the favour of you to show these sand and stones to the Hon. Edward Harrison and Samuel Peak Esquir.

Moses then proceeds to describe how "the rubies and saphirs and topazes at Pegu" are actually mined, ending with a plea to offer his services to these men in any way he can. He adds in closing to "please remember my service to all friends in the coffeehouse." Appended to his letter is a public manifest signed on September 26, 1731 by local diamond merchants testifying to the fact that "Mr. Marcus Moses merchant" was well known to them and that no other "white" merchant (a category in which the Jew Moses is included) was so familiar with the mines themselves. There is no indication whether or not Moses succeeded in selling his precious stones in this instance. He subsequently died in poverty in 1735 although his son Levi continued to run the family business in Madras for another twenty years.[3]

Moses' economic woes were preceded by his political struggles within the Ashkenazic community of London, which had plagued him since the first decade of his arrival. For reasons not entirely clear, Moses dared to challenge the authority of the chief Ashkenazic rabbi of London, Aaron Hart, also known as Uri Phoebus, and indirectly his chief lay supporter and patron, Reb Aberle. On August 27, 1706, Rabbi Hart approved a divorce in a highly secretive manner for a wealthy merchant and gambler named Asher Ensel Cohen, who sought to end his marriage to his first wife. The divorce proceedings were so questionable that Rabbi Hart used the services of the Sephardic scribe rather than his own. Moses had already clashed with Aberle when he had tried unsuccessfully to open a small synagogue in the home of Abraham Nathan, his business colleague. Aberle, who had almost certainly acted with Rabbi Hart's approval, had gone to the local court to block this move, seeing it as a slap in the rabbi's face.

Moses' public protest of the questionable divorce was sure to aggravate their relationship even more. Rabbi Hart responded rashly by excommunicating Moses for daring to question his rabbinic prerogative to issue divorces. The *ḥerem* (writ of excommunication) of Rabenu Tam (c. 1100–71) could be applied as just punishment, so he claimed, for Moses' insubordinate behavior. Just as the medieval sage had violently attacked any scholars who had refused to accept his exclusive authority in matters of Jewish law, so too did Rabbi Hart presumptuously claim a similar status as a legal authority. He had no qualms about the hardship the *ḥerem* would cause Moses and his family, threatening his livelihood through social and economic ostracism from the community. Given the potential ruin that threatened Moses, he turned for rabbinic support elsewhere, first to the Hebrew teacher of his children, Johanan Holleschau, who published his own supporting documents questioning the decree of excommunication. Moses also turned to a brother in Hamburg, who secured the backing of the eminent rabbi of Amsterdam, Ẓevi Ashkenazi, to challenge directly the excessive punishment of Hart. Moses also gained the backing of other rabbis who criticized Hart's impetuous action, including Abraham Rovigo of Jerusalem, who was visiting London at the time. Hart presented his own position in a Hebrew pamphlet published in London in 1707, but Holleschau's more learned publication and Ashkenazi's responsum finally carried the day, bolstered no doubt by the obvious political clout of the Moses family among several powerful rabbis on the Continent.

Moses subsequently completed his break with the chief rabbi by opening a rival synagogue, later known as the Hambro synagogue, along with a plot of land for a cemetery. He installed his loyal friend Holleschau as the synagogue's first rabbi. The conflict, having caused much pain and emotional stress to Marcus Moses and Freudchen, was finally over, although through the reportage of an evangelical deacon in Fürth, who had read the Hebrew accounts of the conflict, it became a minor cause célèbre in the Christian community as well.[4]

Moses' personal troubles appeared to have receded during his long self-imposed exile of six years in India, during which he left the care of his children to his wife in London. It was during this time that his son Moses Marcus grew up and was educated in the Jewish community of London without the personal care of a father during his formative years. It is this period in his life that Moses Marcus recounts in the preface to *The Principal Motives*:

I am descended of a good Family, well known throughout Germany and Poland. My Father and Mother are of the City of Hamburgh, in Germany, and now live in this City (London), in the greatest Splendor imaginable, for private Persons. In the Year 1701 I was born; my Parents took the greatest Care possible of me, and I being their Eldest and first born Son . . . was the more esteemed by them; and especially when I was about eight or nine Years of Age, my Father seeing I took Pleasure in learning my Book, he bestowed a Tutor on me, that when I should come to be master in the Jewish Divinity, I might take Orders. I was quickly ingaged in the Talmuds and Traditions, where all the Jews, who had the Opportunity, know that I apply'd myself to that Study, with some Diligence, and in all those Books, I made such Progress, that I became the Darling of my Father's Heart. When I was about thirteen, my Father went to India, and left me to the particular Care of my Mother, and my tutor, and desired her she would not let me want any Education whatsoever, to qualify me for a Gentleman, and a Scholar, and withal, that I might be sent to Hamburgh, as well for the Accomplishments of a Gentleman, as to study the Jewish divinity.[5]

In other words, several years after the conflict with Rabbi Hart had concluded, in about 1709, Moses Marcus began his formal rabbinical training with a tutor, perhaps the same Johanan Holleschau, or one of his associates. At the time of his bar mitzvah, however, his father left him for India, despite the fact, as Marcus puts it, that he was "the Darling of [his] Father's Heart." This must have constituted quite a blow to him at a very tender age in his development. Despite the advantages of an extensive education and despite a life of material comfort, he appears to have felt deprived. A year later Freudchen sent him to study in Hamburg to continue his rabbinical studies and perhaps to secure the paternal supervision of her brother, who resided in the city.

Moses Marcus studied in Hamburg for the next three years, that is, between 1715 and 1718, at which time he "became well skilled in the Hebrew Language, the French, etc., and several other gentile Qualifications, especially in the Jewish Talmuds and Traditions, so that I was respected by all who knew me." As he explains it, he was still young and "not fit to take Degrees," so when his mother urged him to come home, he responded to her "tender affection" as well as to "several kind Letters from my Father in India." After a year he returned to the Hamburg yeshivah to complete his studies for the lesser rabbinic title *ḥaver.*[6]

At the age of eighteen and having completed a significant part of his course of rabbinic study, he was introduced to "several German Protestant Divines, with whom I conversed and discoursed about Several Differences between the Jewish and Christian Faith." He was initially convinced by some of their arguments but rejected others. In light of their "kind treatment, the Charity and Piety that I found among them," he continued to probe the matter, read the New Testament, and compared it with the Old. He was particularly impressed by how the Old Testament prophecies seemed fulfilled in the New.[7]

In 1721 he was finally reunited with his father, who returned from India with "immense Riches" and embraced him "with all the tender Love and Affection imaginable." He, nevertheless, continued his theological discussions "with several Reverend Divines," who gave him "a farther Insight into the Grounds of Salvation." He attempted to discuss his theological doubts with his father, who soon became impatient with his son's heretical notions and threatened him with fiscal and even bodily harm: "For it would be the Ruin of me, both in Soul and Body, and if I should turn Christian he would not allow me one single Farthing; but would rather spend a hundred thousand Pounds in Law against me, and would also seek Means that I should be destroy'd." Marcus related how his father struck him with a "caseknife" and later offered to arrange for a marriage with a niece from Hamburg with a handsome income. When Marcus continued to speak about "the Truth of the Christian faith, he again threatened to cut off [his] income and the servants who attended to all [his] needs." Moses Marcus's narrative thus underscores the dramatic difference between his spiritual quest and his father's seemingly closed mind. Moses appeared totally incapable of responding to the doubts of his son other than through economic deprivation and physical abuse. Perhaps the son's act of conversion was indeed a way of getting back at his father for the latter's inadequacies in raising and relating to the spiritual needs of his son.[8]

When he finally converted on New Year's Day, 1723, whether the Jewish or the Christian one is unclear from the text, he was forced into a tavern and threatened by his father's associates to be taken to Holland or Germany and "there to turn Jew again," with the additional bribe of a large sum of money. He refused and was vilified by a certain Jew who wished him dead. He survived, nevertheless, because of the kindness of "a worthy Gentleman," with whom he lived, who had assisted him in his "Calamities," and without whom he would have perished.[9]

One final detail is worthy of note in Marcus's revealing narrative. Owing to his conversion he was immediately cut off from the economic support of his parents. This condition forced Marcus "to sue him for a Maintenance, according to Law." He indicates that he was able to prevail upon "several eminent German Jews" to bear witness on his behalf, those in particular who were not dependent on his father's favor. He closes finally with an appeal to the reader to recall his good character "as a Gentleman and a scholar" and reiterates that he only survived because of the aid of the "worthy Gentleman."[10]

Marcus's personal account elicits three major questions, each of which requires elucidation so that we may fully comprehend the circumstances that precipitated his break from Judaism and his personal separation from his family. The first has to do with the initial contacts Marcus had in Hamburg, specifically with the "German Protestant Divines" who were so kind and patient with him during the time of his first inquiries regarding the Christian faith. The second relates to the lawsuit he mentions against his father to force the latter to support him even after his repudiation of his ancestral faith. How was such an action possible and did Marcus succeed in this audacious act? Finally, who was the "Worthy Gentleman" Marcus mentioned twice in his narrative who provided him with both the spiritual and material support to overcome the pain that his separation from family and community obviously engendered? Let us consider carefully each of these three matters.

I have no firm evidence to identify the "German Protestant Divines" Moses Marcus actually met in Hamburg, but three possibilities present themselves. The first is the missionary group originally founded by Esdras Edzard and his sons, which was active in Hamburg at the end of the seventeenth century and the early eighteenth. On the basis of a recent study of this group during the period Marcus was in Hamburg, it seems most unlikely that they could have inspired and persuaded such an elite intellectual as Marcus to consider the Christian faith. Their outreach was to the poor, uneducated, and desolate. Their teachers do not seem to fit the profile Marcus offers. The second possibility is the pietists or other religious non-conformists active in Altona or Hamburg at the time, who might have shown interest in this young man and offered him "charity and piety," in contrast to the orthodox Lutherans of Hamburg, who would probably have been indifferent to the mission of the Jews. Such groups included Chiliasts such as Oliger Pauli and his disciples, or the former Mennonite charismatic preacher Jakob Denner, or the disciple of Jakob Boehme, Johann Otto Glusing. The third possibility is Anglicans residing in Hamburg, members of the "court of the Right Worshipful Company of the Merchant Adventurers" who lived in the so-called Englisches Haus on Groeningerstrasse in Hamburg's Neustadt. These English merchants were allowed to practice the Anglican faith and to employ their own preacher, who beginning in 1719 was Dr. John Thomas. Thomas was not a German divine, but he did know German.[11]

Of all these possibilities, I would probably opt for the last one for several reasons. Marcus was a native English speaker. His time in Hamburg was spent in the yeshivah—most likely the yeshivah in neighboring Altona, which was under the direction of Rabbi Yeḥezkel Katzenellenbogen—not in the university. And even though he knew German and French, he might have been more comfortable in English or Yiddish. Meeting Englishmen in Hamburg might have been a pleasant and comfortable occasion for him. A light conversation might have created the opportunity for more serious theological discussion. Since his ultimate destination became the Anglican Church, this avenue seems to have been the most practical and the most compatible with the social relations he was realistically capable of forming.[12]

As to the lawsuit Marcus initiated against his father, no speculation is necessary because the documentation regarding his initiative, at least through most of the 1720s, still exists in the records of the High Court of the Chancery, held today in the Public Record Office of London. Marcus's recourse to a law obliging his father to support him even after his conversion to Christianity refers to a bill passed in 1702 under the reign of Queen Anne entitled "An Act to Oblige the Jews to Maintain and Provide for Their Protestant Children."[13]

The first mention of the suit is recorded by Thomas Earl of Macclesfield on January 25, 1722 regarding "the Maintenance of a Protestant Son of a Jew, Petition of Moses Marcus, the son of a Jew, alleging that he has embraced the Protestant religion, and that his father refuses him maintenance in consequence." The circumstances of the petitioner and his father are then carefully delineated, including the fact that his father had "a plentifull estate and lives in great repute and esteeme in the City of London." The court considered Moses Marcus to be a twenty-two-year-old adult of sound mind capable of making the decision to convert, "being by such education become capable of judging of the true religion and having diligently searched the Scriptures and inquired into the Christian religion as well as the Jewish and being fully convinced of the Truth of the one and of the errors of the other." In his newly converted state, Marcus found himself "hated and scorned by his parents and cast off by his said father, and in order to compel him to exchange his religion is by his father refused to be allowed a fitting maintenance suitable to the degree and ability of his said father." Since Marcus had only learned to be "a gentleman and a scholar," without his father's support he was now destitute and incapable of earning his own living.[14]

The document then cites the act of Parliament of 1702 compelling a Jewish parent to support his Christian child. The father is requested to appear before the judge so that he can decide "what he thinks fitting to be allowed yearly for the maintenance of the petitioner," and, in the meantime, the father is to deposit five thousands pounds for security, and fifty for his son's clothing expenses.[15]

A similar document dated February 17, 1726, orders Marcus's father to pay his son sixty pounds per annum. Marcus again claimed that he had received no support whatsoever from his father, who had apparently avoided the requested payments to that point. Complicating the matter was the father's counterclaim that his son "returned to the Jewish worship and professed himself to be a Jew and kept the then Passover with Jews, and as soon as the same was over voluntarily went over to Holland and there renounced the Christian religion and went publickly to the synagogue and did penance for his having turned Christian in England and continued in Holland a year and five months and behaved as a Jew all that time. . . ." As a Jew, the father claimed, he provided his son with his proper maintenance. Marcus, however, denied the fact that he was anything other than a Christian.[16]

In addition to the Chancery proceedings, a series of depositions taken from witnesses supporting the father are extant. These are from Ashkenazic Jewish merchants living in Amsterdam and obvious associates of Marcus Moses. The documents, mostly dated 1728, are written in low Dutch accompanied by English translations. They attempt to reconstruct the whereabouts and activities of Moses Marcus precisely at the time when his father claimed he had reverted to Judaism, in 1724–25. They seek to ascertain how Moses Marcus financed his room and board, whether through his father's support or not. Each of the witnesses testifies to having paid Marcus specific sums advanced to him at the direction of his father. So, for example, Marcus Solomon Levy, a twenty-one-year-old merchant living in the city of Amsterdam appeared as a witness on behalf of Marcus Moses. Being a contemporary of Marcus the son, Levy knew him most of his life both in London and in Amsterdam. On or about December, 1724, "the said Moses Marcus came to live and board with him . . . for about the space of one year and he did lodge, eat, and drink with the Depousul and his family." During this time, Levy explicitly states, Marcus Moses thanked him "for having taken his son to board in his house and he the said Marcus Moses would satisfy and pay his boarding." Parenthetically, the document inserts a note that the father refused to take an oath on the English Bible but would only take one on the "Sopher [sic] Torah," "which shows the great regard he has for the originall language."[17]

Marcus Moses' claim that his son had returned to the Jewish faith, at least temporarily while in Amsterdam, was not only supported by these witnesses who had opened their homes to Moses, had provided him with finances, and had even celebrated the Jewish holidays with him. It was also confirmed by a remarkable letter located in the British Library written by Moses Marcus to his parents from Amsterdam on May 2, 1724. The critical lines read as follows: "I hope you will pardon ye folly I committed. I never had Committed it if several people had not perswaded me to it telling me by turning Christian I could oblige you to give me a Sum of Money but as I was born a Jew so I will Die a Jew. I go here to Sinagogue and live as a Jew ought to do so I hope God Almighty will pardon my sins." He asks their forgiveness for not saying more in this short letter, but because of his "great consternation and fatigue" he cannot continue and promises to write more later. He closes: "I remain until Death your most dutifull and most obedient son Moses Marcus."[18]

In the court record of 1727, a new element accompanies the recurrent requests of the court to secure the father's payments for his destitute son: "[Marcus Moses] . . . is by reason of great losses and misfortunes we have come upon him in the way of his trade become insolvent and is indebted to other persons of his creed . . . and is unable to pay them by which he has nothing to support himself and wife and eight children who are unprovided for so that he is not able any longer to pay this allowance of 60 per annum to his son Moses Marcus for his maintenance." In light of the father's bankruptcy, the court suspended the payment to his son "so as not to remain any longer a charge on his estate." In a final court document dated 1730, we read that "Moses Marcus still demands back payments not made to him from Christmas 1723 to February 1726 and in 1726–27," that is, prior to the time his father declared he was bankrupt. This is the last record of this long and protracted legal proceeding.[19]

The court's acknowledgment of Marcus Moses' insolvency matches precisely the other evidence we have of his financial condition by the late 1720s. As mentioned previously, Moses was obliged to return to India in 1728 in order to try to recover his losses, which had transformed him from a highly affluent man to a penniless one in only a relatively brief span of some six or seven years. It is clear that his son's recourse to the courts was also a reflection of the son's economic distress and his constant need to support himself and his own family, if indeed he was married by this time. It seems, however, that the son gained little from his constant legal actions. While still affluent, Marcus Moses had enough influence and personal connections to avoid paying his son the amounts stipulated by the courts, and ultimately he was excused from these payments because of his own economic downturn. Neither party benefited in the end from these public displays of mutual recrimination on the part of either the father or the son.

Even more significant than the economic aspects of the court records is their revelation of Marcus's obvious ambivalence about his conversion. During his sojourn in Amsterdam immediately after his English book was published, and during the time he may have been in touch with his Dutch publisher, who would soon put out a revised and enlarged version of his book in Dutch,[20] Moses clearly lived among Jewish merchants and their families whom he had apparently known since his childhood. With the blessing and directives of his father, they supported him and opened their homes to him. In writing to his parents at precisely this time to insist that he was still Jewish, Moses merely confirmed what the court depositions had documented. He had indeed experienced a "relapse," whether temporary or not, and was reconsidering his new lifestyle as a Christian. The legal documents seem to indicate that he ultimately reclaimed his

Christian identity, even though the circumstances of his eventual return to the church are not known. Be that as it may, the resolute language by which he affirmed his loyalty to the Anglican Church in the preface to *The Principal Motives* needs to be tempered by the reality of family, social, and economic pressures he undoubtedly faced both in London and Amsterdam in the years immediately following his conversion and the publication of his testimony. As we shall see, despite the absence of any additional evidence of future "relapses" to his former faith, his subsequent life and career consistently reflected his ambivalence and conflicted identity as a new Christian with still noticeably positive feelings about Jews and Judaism.

Our final question concerning Marcus's account of his life leading up to the conversion regards the identity of "the Worthy Gentleman" who offered him both material sustenance and spiritual support at a critical time when his parents had turned against him. I have no conclusive evidence, but I propose strongly that this man was the Anglican cleric who was responsible for Moses Marcus's conversion in the first place, David Wilkins (1685–1745). The key document pointing to a connection between the two is the affidavit testifying to Marcus's credentials as a worthy candidate for conversion into the Anglican Church, which was written by Wilkins on August 10, 1723 and published on the first page of Moses' book. Wilkins signed this note with his full title: "Chaplain to his grace the Lord Archbishop of Canterbury." He is quite explicit about this relationship with Moses Marcus and offers a clear portrait of what attracted the church to this young man in the first place:

That I, whose name is Underwritten, do personally know, and have frequently conversed with Mr. Moses Marcus, and find him a pious, sober, and ingenious young Man, very well versed in the Hebrew, Chaldaic, Talmudical, and Rabbinical, Learning, far beyond any Body that ever I knew of his Age and Education. Besides this knowledge, and that of the English Tongue; he has also, in his Travels, made himself Master of the German and French languages; and has now by the assisting Grace of God, attained to a very good Knowledge of the Gospel Dispensation, and of his Duty as a Christian, which he has now a proper Opportunity to exercise, in thanking his cruel Parents for the good Education they have given him, and for the Improvements, which by their Care, he has made in the Jewish learning; the Deficiency, and blind Superstition of which, has been the principal Motive of his Conversion to Christianity.[21]

Wilkins testifies to the exceptional rabbinic education Marcus received, even giving due credit to his "cruel Parents" for this achievement. Furthermore, Wilkins deems this an asset, a considerable accomplishment, for a candidate for conversion to Christianity. He also singles out Marcus's knowledge of English, as well as German and French, which explain Moses' ability to converse with "German Protestant Divines" without any difficulty, if in fact, that was the case. Wilkins did not mention Marcus's ability to read Latin, which he may have acquired later; but that ability is obvious in light of his later English translation of a Latin tome. In short, Wilkins testified that Moses Marcus was no ordinary convert. His education both in Judaism and in languages demonstrated his scholarly proclivities. Wilkins, as we shall see, was himself a scholar with expertise in these same disciplines. He was a most appropriate cleric to show interest in Marcus precisely because Marcus was a young man of his own liking and in his own image, that of an academic clergyman.

Marcus repaid Wilkins the compliment in his own dedication of the volume, written to none other than William Wake, "the Archbishop of Canterbury and Metropolitan of All England," and Wilkins's own supervisor and patron. Marcus focused again on the painful circumstances of leaving his family to embrace the church and on the kindness he received from one of his Christian mentors, most likely Wilkins himself:

I am banished from that [his family] of my natural Parents, once most endearing and indulgent Parents, who spared for nothing of their precious Treasures, wherewith they abound, to make me Great and Happy in this World; but have now conceived a mortal Hatred to me, upon the Account of this religious Difference; and deny me Bread to eat and Rainment to put on. By whom being rejected, I quickly found myself like a shipwrack'd Man, plunged in an Ocean of Hardships, under which, in all human Appearance, I had utterly sunk, had not one of my Susceptors in Baptism, with the greatest Tenderness, took me under his Roof, where he still continues to entertain me, and supports me with the Necessaries of Life.

It seems reasonable to assume that the warmth and enthusiasm Wilkins displayed in his introduction of Moses Marcus matches the affection the young acolyte appears to offer here.[22]

One more remark in Marcus's dedication to the archbishop is worthy of comment as it might relate to Wilkins and his role in the church as Wake's personal chaplain, a position totally dependent on the good graces of his employer. Marcus surprisingly interjects a note of concern, hardly relevant to his own personal conversion but most relevant to the clergy sponsoring his candidacy to the church. It follows his own personal affirmation of his belief that there is a "state of Happiness after Death" and that faith in Jesus Christ is absolutely necessary to attain immortal life. He then adds:

I am sorry to find many, who call themselves Christians, of a contrary Opinion. From such Men as these, young Proselytes, in my Circumstances, must expect but a cold Welcome to Christian Communion. But we will not be disheartened by the Slights of these Libertines, while we see a Patriarch at the Head of the Church of England, who stands ready, with open Arms, to receive us into that Way of Salvation, wherein he leads us by his own shining Example; and zealously performs

that Promise of our Lord, that when our natural Friends disown us, and perse-
cute us for his Names sake, we shall find compassionate nursing Fathers of his
Church, who will make up this Loss to us.[23]

How interesting, indeed, that the astute Moses Marcus should conflate
the issue of disbelief in divine immortality and "the Slights of the Libertines" with the affections tendered him by a "compassionate nursing"
father of the Church in the person of David Wilkins! One might interpret this unusual gesture of flattery as a not so inconspicuous effort at
thanking his kind mentor by bolstering his public image in the church's
fight against heresy. At the very least, it signals and pays high compliment to Wilkins's particular concern and approach to the mission of
the church and to his interest in proselytizing, a matter to which we will
return shortly.

Who was this David Wilkins to whom Moses Marcus was unstinting in
his praise? Wilkins was born to Prussian parents living in Memel, Lithuania, with the original name of Wilke. It is unclear how he received his
extensive education in ancient Semitic languages. He once mentioned
Ezekiel Spanheim, the elector of Brandenburg's ambassador in England,
as a former teacher. In an anonymous biographical portrait appended
to the manuscripts of his sermons housed in the Bodleian Library, additional details appear. His father, who was a justice and also a merchant
in England and Holland, and his mother, who was called by the English
name of Catherine Murray, afforded him private tutors in his home until
they sent him to the University of Köningsberg, where he attained the
degree of master of arts.[24]

After extensive travels through Poland, Lithuania, Germany, and Holland, Wilkins arrived in Oxford in 1707. Over the years, he involved
himself in several scholarly projects, including a history of the patriarchs
of Alexandria, an edition of the Coptic New Testament, an edition of
the Targum on Chronicles, an Armenian version of the third epistle of
Corinthians, and the new polyglot edition of the Lord's Prayer, whose
general editor was John Chamberlyne. He also worked on a translation
of parts of Maimonides' *Mishneh Torah* that remains in manuscript. In
1709, he again left for the Continent, but he returned to London in 1711,
where he converted from the Lutheran Church to the Anglican Church
through the mentorship of John More, the bishop of Ely. In this, he followed the path of one of his intellectual patrons and fellow Prussian
immigrant, John Ernst Grabe.[25]

Several years prior to Wilkins's contact with Marcus in 1716, William
Wake collated Wilkins to the rectory of Mongeham Parva and Great Chart
in Kent and made him his librarian and eventually his domestic chaplain
as well. He was later collated to the rectory of Hadleigh and Monks Eligh
in Suffolk. Eventually Wake, his patron, appointed him the archbishop

of Suffolk in the very room of the "very learned" Dr. Humphrey Prideaux on January 1, 1721. How symbolic that Wilkins was personally linked to Prideaux, only three years before the latter's death in 1724!

Wake employed Wilkins in a variety of scholarly projects, which included an edition of the Anglo-Saxon laws, the complete works of John Selden, an edition of the Coptic Pentateuch, and especially the *Consilia Magnae Britanniae et Hiberniea,* on the history of the English Church councils in four volumes. Perhaps as a result of his incredible output of publications, Wilkins was often criticized for his sloppy scholarship, his misuse of manuscripts, and his linguistic mistakes in Coptic, Anglo-Saxon, Hebrew, and Arabic. John Gagnier, the professor of Arabic studies at Oxford, criticized his knowledge of Semitic languages. Thomas Hearn, the librarian of the Bodleian, referred to him as "a vain ambitious man, of little judgment, tho' great industry." Wilkins was ultimately denied a degree in Oxford and accused of being a spy, of living off the kindness of others, and of marrying the half-witted Margaret Fairfax, the eldest sister of Lord Thomas Fairfax, for her money. He was obliged to turn to Cambridge, where he finally received the degree of doctor of divinity through the intervention of Richard Bentley, the Regius Professor of Divinity, in 1717.[26]

A more favorable image of Wilkins is offered through an extensive reading of his many extant sermons, including the only one of which that was actually printed at the time, a sermon Wilkins originally preached in Lambeth Chapel, London in 1722. Already in this latter sermon, it is evident the degree to which Wilkins displayed a mastery of Jewish sources. Using as his scriptural passage Deut. 33:8, Moses' blessing to the tribe of Levi, Wilkins finds it equally applicable to the "Ministers of the Gospel," that is, the bishops, priests, and deacons of the Anglican Church. Preaching in honor of the consecration of the lord bishop of Chichester before a significant clerical audience, Wilkins had no compunction in citing the Babylonian Talmud, Isaac Abravanel, Baḥya ben Asher, Joseph ibn Yaḥya, Moses Maimonides, and David Kimḥi. On the contrary, he openly acknowledged his appropriation of Jewish sources to elicit his Christian homiletic message, adding at one point: "From hence we may observe what even a Jewish expositor had done before that this Thummim and Urim, this perfection and illumination, was one of the divine Gifts and Graces of the Holy Ghost."[27]

Ten volumes of Wilkins's sermons are located in the Bodleian Library. Like the printed sermon, they consistently reveal a broad erudition in Jewish sources, especially rabbinical texts and medieval exegesis. In one sermon, he discusses Josephus's description of the Pharisees and compares them with the Stoics.[28] In another, on the theme of the antiquity of the Sabbath, he refers to Philo, who calls the Sabbath the birthday of the world and the universal feast. In the same sermon, Wilkins elaborates on the meaning of circumcision among the Jews.[29] In another, he offers one of his few disparaging remarks on ancient Judaism, commenting on the hypocrisy of the Pharisees, "Saints in Garb and Dress, but abominably wicked and polluted in their Hearts."[30] In yet another on the ceremony of hand washing among the Jews, which he attributes to King Solomon, he offers a impressive list of Jewish legal references, including those taken from Joseph Karo's *Shulkhan Arukh* and his *Kesef Mishnah,* Morechai Yaffe's *Levush,* Jacob ben Asher's *Arba'ah Turim,* and Maimonides' *Mishneh Torah.*[31]

Wilkins returns to the theme of the sins of the Pharisees in another sermon, this time conflating the scribes and Pharisees with the Catholics in Rome.[32] In interpreting the story of the binding of Isaac in Genesis 22, in another sermon, he cites "a Talmudic Book called *Pirke Eliezer,* chap. 31," along with Philo's *Life of Abraham,* and Josephus's *Wars.*[33] Elsewhere he refers to the *Targum* ("The Chaldaic Paraphrases"), which supports his Christian messianic reading of biblical verses.[34] He also discusses the analogy between the Jewish Passover and the Last Supper.[35] In a sermon based on Lev. 19:17, he adds: "These words have been the occasion of one of the wisest Observations, learned Compilers of the Jewish Talmud made upon the Moral Precepts of the law. They grounded the Discipline of reproving their Neighbour upon the words of my Text." And in the same homily, he continues: "The Jews had so right a sense of the Necessity of fraternal Reproof that a learned Rabbi ascribed the Reason of the Destruction of Jerusalem to the Wanton Neglect of it."[36] Another sermon offers a learned discussion of the Pharisaic notion of the resurrection of the dead. Wilkins accepted the fact that they had such a notion, "but [the Pharisees] knew not, how to explain the Nature and Manner of it." Wilkins cites Josephus in support of their belief in the immortality of the soul, but claims that they mentioned "not a word" that he was "as yet sensible of, of the restoration of the dead Body from Corruption," a position voiced coincidently by Humphrey Prideaux.[37]

What is clear from even this brief overview of Wilkins's extensive homiletic writings is that he was comfortable with Jewish texts of all varieties, including legal ones. He demonstrated this knowledge only on those occasions when his subject merited it. Many of the themes of his sermons had little to do with Judaism. He was much more obsessed with English politics and support of the king of England, with the crimes of the papists and Jesuits, with Protestant martyrdom, and with criticizing the Socinians and other heretical groups.[38] He has no particular bone to pick with Judaism. Even in the few instances in which he criticizes the Pharisees, he is not necessarily thinking about contemporary Jews. In fact, he more readily equates them with papists, as we have seen. His Jewish knowledge, in short, appears to be part of his makeup as a clergyman and scholar. He does not show it off nor is he obsessed with it, either positively or negatively. It is just there, to be enlisted when making a point.

Nevertheless, it seems clear that in meeting up with so formidable a Christian scholar of Judaism, Marcus had truly found an ideal mentor to lead him out of Judaism, a true Christian Hebraist with a deep appreciation of the texts and ideas Moses Marcus had studied throughout his life. Wilkins was the embodiment of that fusion Marcus sought in appreciating deeply the Jewish heritage while still finding ultimate truth in the Christian faith. And Wilkins could not have failed to enjoy the company of his young neophyte in the study of Christianity, with whom he could converse about subjects of shared knowledge and interest. One is tempted to go farther in speculating about the source of Wilkins's profound familiarity with Judaism. Was he himself a convert? Did his Prussian origins obscure a previous Jewish identity? Might the accusations of his harshest critics regarding his being a foreigner, his arrogance, and his mercenary nature somehow betray a secret Jewish past? I might be far off the mark in even proposing such a possibility if not for one recurrent pattern that appears throughout Wilkins's sermons, indeed, throughout other manuscripts he wrote. He inserts repeatedly into his texts a Hebrew acronym that might be pronounced "Ami Asu" and when spelled out refers to Ps. 121:2, *Ezri me'im Adonai oseh shamayim va arez* ("My help comes from the Lord, the creator of the heavens and the earth"). As best I can determine, it is his special way of signing the text. Furthermore, these handwritten Hebrew letters, along with his others, reveal a handwriting so natural as to suggest that it was acquired at a young age and was not simply the later attainment of a mature scholar. Be that as it may, I am not yet prepared to conclude that the scribbler who repeatedly jotted down his favorite Hebrew acronym throughout the pages of his English-language manuscripts was sending a coded signal about who he actually was. But the thought is still tempting![39]

Finally, I would like to consider one additional bit of evidence on David Wilkins and his connection with Moses Marcus, perhaps the most interesting of all. In a letter Moses Marcus wrote to Sir Hans Sloane in 1737, to be discussed more fully in the next chapter, Marcus lists all of the books he had published and those in manuscript that were "now in press." At the top of the list of books not yet published is the following title: "The Prayers of the Jews in their Synagogues for Common Days, Sabbaths, New Moons, Feasts and Fasts throughout the whole Year, to which will be added: 1. The Prayers of the Ancient Jews and their Sacrifices in the Temple Collected from the Mishna and Talmud. 2. The ancient and modern Customs of the Jews at their Feasts and Fasts. 3. Perke Aboth, or the Moral and Philosophical Sayings of the Ancient Sages about

Three Hundred Years before Christ."[40] Despite Marcus's assurance that in 1737 the work was "now in press," I have never located such a volume. It is unclear whether the original work, if it did exist, included the three parts or whether this was simply wishful thinking on his part. We will have an opportunity to examine the rest of Marcus's writing in due course.

In the catalogue of the Egerton manuscripts located in the British Library, the following entry describes Egerton Ms. 792: "Jewish liturgy and prayers, translated into English by Dr. David Wilkins." The cataloguer indicates that the manuscript was written by Wilkins himself.[41] Having studied the manuscript carefully, I do not think that Wilkins was the author, but believe that Moses Marcus was, and that this is the text, or a version of the text, that Marcus had in mind when he indicated to Sir Hans Sloane that he had translated the Jewish liturgy. Nevertheless, Wilkins had a personal stake in this composition which led the cataloguer to identify him as the author. I would like to propose that Marcus undertook this translation of the Jewish liturgy at Wilkin's request, and that as a kind of celebration of his protégé's achievement, Wilkins wrote the homily that concludes the manuscript, which directly alludes to Moses Marcus himself.

The manuscript is missing its entire first section and begins with page 91. It commences at the end of the Friday night service with the *Kiddush,* the washing of the hands, the blessing over the bread, *zemirot* (Hebrew chants at the meal), and grace after the meal. The Sabbath morning prayer follows, including the priestly blessing, a prayer for "the king's majesty," "a song in the Chaldai composed by Rabbi Isaac Luria," and the morning blessing over the wine, followed by the instruction that "the man of the house gives every one that sits at the table a piece of bread." This is followed by the Sabbath afternoon prayer, the *Havdalah* service, with specific instructions differentiating the customs pertaining to Jews living in German lands from those living in Poland. A prayer of protection against demons is included: "I conjure all ye spirits, all ye ghosts, demons, all ye satans, and adversaries . . . that ye shall not touch me . . . from all souls of wicked spirits, from all turbulent demons." Other customs, especially Ashkenazic ones, are delineated, including those associated with the Kabbalah of Isaac Luria.[42]

Other instructions are offered throughout. For example, on the holiday of Hoshana Rabba, "it is a custom of all pious people to stay up all night . . . , reading the law, prophets, and the holy part of the oral law, and cabalistical books, especially the book of Zoar in the chapter of the creation of the world."[43] Similarly, for the holiday of Passover, this comment for the four questions appears: "Note, the following questions and answers are for the Jews to know their chief foundation of religion." The *Ḥad Gadya* prayer is explained in this manner: "The following parable is a mysterie. The Jews being in a persecuting country could not name the nation who should be destroyed so metamorphosed it in other beasts like unto nations who should be destroyed."[44]

The composition includes a translation of the first *mishnah* of *Pirke Avot,* a part of the Yom Kippur liturgy, evening prayers for the second and seventh nights of Passover, and for Shevuot, Succot, and Simhat Torah.[45] At this point the translation breaks off with the terse announcement that the first part is ended. Even a cursory examination of this incomplete manuscript suggests some initial observations. This was part of a much larger work of translation that included the entire *maḥzor,* that is, the Sabbath and festivals liturgy for the entire yearly cycle. It was written by someone who was familiar with local customs, especially Ashkenazic ones, and was also conversant with kabbalistic prayers, including the abjuration of demons and spirits, and other folk customs. Furthermore, complete lines written in Hebrew script suggest the possibility that the writer was a Jew. On the basis of these characteristics, and given the correspondence with what is here and with what Moses Marcus claimed he had done, it seems quite plausible that he was the translator of this unfinished work. If this hypothesis is correct, Moses Marcus was responsible for one of the first translations of the Jewish liturgy into English, albeit an [unfinished?] one, some sixty years before David Levi published his famous editions of both the Ashkenazic and Sephardic prayer books.[46]

On the last page of the manuscript, broken off from the rest of the text and in a slightly different hand, a homily on Matt. 23:15 appears: "Woe unto your Scribes and Pharisees . . ." in a form reminiscent of David Wilkins's other sermons but bearing no resemblance to any of them. Here the author interprets Jesus's rebuke of the scribes as a condemnation of "their horrid hypocricy, their uncharitableness, their barbarity to widows and orphans. . . ." The Pharisees, the author admits, had high standards of piety, but they could not live up to them: "they were of a haughty proud and imperious conduct every one of them striving to overmatch his neighbor in pride and hypocrisie." On account of these sins, the Temple was destroyed and they were scattered all over the face of the earth, and "to this day bare the ignominy of their fathers' heinous sins and transgressions."[47]

The author acknowledges, however, one fine attribute of these scribes: their desire to seek converts, that is, "bringing an ignorant and stupid heathen under the protection of the blessed God, which indeed must be so; it is no less than saving a Soul from eternal perdition and misery." But their noble intentions were spoiled by their purpose and design, which was for self-adulation rather than the glory of God. Moreover, in converting the pagan to their religion, they were making his bad situation even worse: "For at the time of his paganisme and heathenisme he might have been stupid, ignorant and innocent," but "seeing their way of life, living to the height of hypocrisie and pride," he soon imitated their pernicious example.[48]

Yet despite the unfortunate results, the talmudic ideal of equating the *ger*, the stranger, with the proselyte, of giving him food and clothing, and loving him, is still praiseworthy: "God has set a great value upon sincere proselytes or those that shall shelter under the shadow of his divine presence." This stands in contrast, however, with the reluctance of the Jews to welcome converts as stated in the Talmud. This stark contradiction between God's delight in welcoming the stranger and the Jewish inhibition vis-à-vis proselytization demonstrates for the author of the homily the weakness and feebleness of the Talmud. The contradiction is absurd since God always rejoices in the turning of the sinner away from his sins. The Talmud thus contradicts the Holy Scripture as Moses authorized in the book of Deuteronomy.[49]

The homily quickly comes to a close with the following bullet-like conclusions: "But let me return to my text which I shall discourse upon the following heads: How far our duty extends to bring the Jews into our Holy Faith that they may be partakers of heavenly bliss, and we be acquitted of our dutie to God. 2. When we have received them into our communities what our duty is in what manner to instruct and assist them. 3. What benefits we shall reap of such a glorious Jew." The homily abruptly concludes without any development of these three points, which appear to be an outline of what was to follow but was never completed.[50]

My speculation that Moses Marcus translated the prayers contained in the manuscript appears to be strengthened by the unfinished homily that follows it. Wilkins most likely wrote the unfinished sermon as a token of appreciation for his talented student and out of a sense of vindication that his efforts at reaching out to him had not been in vain. He may also have added the homily to legitimize the translation in the first place. The homily well illustrates Wilkins's mixture of appreciation and contempt for the Pharisaic tradition, of welcoming the proselyte but not actively seeking his conversion. What is most revealing is how the object of proselytizing abruptly shifts in the very end from the pagan to the Jew. Who else could the author have meant besides Moses Marcus in extolling the benefits of converting so glorious a member of the Jewish faith?

Chapter 3

The Career of Moses Marcus in London: An Expert on Judaism and a Defender of Religious Orthodoxy

Reconstructing the rest of Moses Marcus's life in the aftermath of his conversion in 1723 and the prolonged financial struggle with his father that lasted at least until 1727 becomes obviously more difficult without the rich narratives his book and court proceedings provide. Nevertheless, considerable evidence does exist to gain a general sense of his life at least through the next decade. In addition to the precious testimonies of others about him, his own writings, both printed and in manuscript, convey considerably more about the ups and downs of his career, his self-image, and the figure he cut among the Christians who came to know him.

Besides the names of his brothers and sisters and those of his many uncles and aunts listed in the family tree of Glikl of Hameln, which was reconstructed in the early Yiddish edition of her autobiography, little is known about Marcus's immediate family. He had six brothers: Hyam or Hyman, Henry, Levy, Samuel, Lipman or Leffman, and Joseph. He also had three sisters: Elizabeth, Hester or Esther, and Susannah. His brothers were all merchants like their father; several of them spent considerable time in India running the family business through much of the eighteenth century. As of 1937, Henry Moses' grave was identifiable at the Hoxton cemetery of the Hambro synagogue.[1]

There is nothing to indicate that Moses Marcus maintained contact with any of his relatives either in London or in Hamburg after he ultimately assumed a Christian identity and after the obviously hurtful feelings the court proceedings engendered. We do know that he was married but know virtually nothing about his wife. She is mentioned in several of the letters written during Marcus's repeated confinements in debtors' prison at the end of the 1730s, letters I shall consider shortly. In a recent genealogical table published in 1999, Marcus's wife is listed as Judith Isaac, the daughter of Benjamin Isaac, also known as Wolf Prager, but this is most likely a mistake.[2]

We are on more solid ground when we examine several notices of Marcus within English Christian society over a span of some ten years beginning in 1729. This is also the same period in which he published his remaining works, which, in turn, garnered some attention from several distinguished Christian contemporaries. What is clear from this limited evidence is that all of his contacts, at least those mentioned in our sources, are within Christian society. After his extended visit to Amsterdam in 1724–25, it appears that his interactions with Jews came to an end.

One of the first references to Marcus's whereabouts in London in the late 1720s is found in the private journal of John Byrom (1692–1763), a writer and stenographer known for his invention of a special system for taking shorthand. Byrom was also a member of an elite social group that included the likes of Dr. Richard Bentley, Bishop Benjamin Hoadley, William Whiston, Anthony Collins, Conyers Middleton, William Law, and many others.[3]

Byrom was particularly interested in the Hebrew language and spent considerable time seeking out experts who could answer his many queries. In this context he first heard about Moses Marcus from an associate named Dr. Hooper (perhaps Dr. Francis Hooper?) on December 5, 1729 at Trinity College. Several weeks later, on December 31, 1729 in London, he recorded the following lines: "Had much talk with Moses Marcus last night at Richards about Hebrew; he said the present letters were the old ones, and quoted [Adonai] and his book against Whiston, which I promised to buy of him, and Selah, being a contraction of three words, begins the words of the song=da. Capo. Canticles=the Captivity, Cabala; Abraham wrote as well as Moses; promised to buy his book, which I have." In the next entry he mentions visiting Richards, I assume a tavern of sorts, again on January 5, 1730, but Marcus was not mentioned.[4]

Marcus's translation of Johann Gottlob Carpzov's critique of William Whiston, to be discussed at length below, had been published earlier in the same year, and it is obvious that Marcus was proud of this work and wanted to sell it. Byrom's other comments are cryptic and not fully comprehensible, although the general gist of the conversation about the authenticity of Hebrew Scripture preserved by the Jews is clear and well relates to Whiston's accusations about its unreliability. But beyond the comments themselves is the actual scene of an English gentleman, not quite a scholar but with scholarly pretensions and dilettante interests in biblical and Hebraic studies, chatting with Marcus in a London pub about Hebrew grammar and other related matters. Byrom's casual conversation with Marcus needs to be seen in the context of his records of several other discussions with Jews, including Israel Lyons in 1733,[5] and another Jew called Moses Beharer in 1734. In his second conversation with Lyons, Byrom reports that they drank tea and read a Hebrew book together, and that he told Lyons "of a black Jew that had a book with points from Cochin, China [sic]."[6] Byrom's testimony about his informal conversations with converted Jews such as Moses Marcus and with Jews such as Lyons provides some sense of an interest in Hebrew studies in the larger public sphere of London's society, far beyond the more scholarly forums of Hebraic scholarship. The portrait of Marcus enjoying a social evening at Richards in the company of an English socialite and discussing Hebrew roots marks the special ambiance of English society in the early eighteenth century.

A less flattering portrait of Moses Marcus is offered some seven years later by John Perceval (1683–1748), the first earl of Egmont, in his diary. Perceval was a wealthy man who had become active in English politics by the 1720s. Later, together with James Oglethorpe, he was involved in the founding of the English colony in Georgia. He supervised the publication of his diaries in 1742, which reveal a rich portrait of his social and cultural world, as well as a taste of his pomposity.[7]

In the entry to his diary of Tuesday, June 1, 1736, he writes the following: "I went to town in the morning and dined at home. In the evening, I went to the Wood Street Counter to relieve Moses Marcus, a converted Jew, whom Smith the engraver has cast into prison . . . because he was not paid for the copper plates of the book Marcus is publishing. Moses said five guineas would get him out, which I gave him. This poor man has a family to subsist, and nothing to live on, but teaching languages and composing books relating to the Jewish religion, which he is well qualified for understanding his own Hebrew, Latin, Italian, and English."[8]

Perceval's description of Marcus confirms what we already know about him and adds a few details. There is mention of a family, probably meaning children in addition to Marcus's wife. His language skills have grown to include Latin and Italian, in addition to the German and French mentioned earlier by Wilkins. He earns a living by writing books on Judaism as well as teaching languages, which might mean others in addition Hebrew. The incident also reveals the instability of Marcus's career, as well as his ability to call on wealthy associates such as Perceval for assistance. From the context it is clear that Perceval was quite familiar with him and did not hesitate to help him when asked.

Only a year later Marcus was again in trouble and this time he turned to another affluent and influential member of London's elite society, Sir Hans Sloane (1660–1753).[9] In this case, his begging letter is preserved without a hint of a response from Sloane, so it is hard to assess whether the two men had any social contact prior to the occasion that prompted this letter. Whether Marcus knew Sloane well or not, he invested considerable energy in composing this letter, introducing himself and his work and revealing quite remarkably many of his social contacts. He composed the letter on August 16, 1737 in Wood Street Counter, the same debtor's prison from which John Perceval had bailed him out only a year earlier.

It is so important for reconstructing Moses Marcus's life, writings, and social network that it needs to be cited in full:

I am willing to hope your Honour's extensive Goodness will pardon this Presumption. As it is my great Misfortune to be upwards of sixteen months confined in this loathsome and wretched place, for a Debt my wife contracted, labouring under the most extreme difficulties of life; scarce anything to cover my naked nose; upon the brink of perishing; almost devoured of Vermin, by which means my body is full of sores and blotches, a most dismal spectacle to behold! If your Honour be pleased to send any person to inspect into my unhappy condition, must be shock'd and estonished at my dismal and frightful appearance.

I am willing to hope, as I have been serviceable to the Publick by my knowledge in several Oriental and Modern Languages as is well known to several eminent Persons, whom I have had the Honour to teach; especially to his Grace the Duke of Mountague, who, together with the Earl of Egmont, the Lord Bishops of London, Winchester, Litchfield and Coventry and some charitably Disposed Gentlemen, have largely contributed towards my Enlargement so that there remains about fifty shillings for fees and incident charges for whom I have translated several pieces in the oriental languages, when the present Interpreter to His Majesty could not translate them, and I received a handsome gratuity for the same. Likewise when I confuted the objections of the late modern Free Thinkers or Infidels, to the entire satisfaction of the learned Divines and received their thanks for the same, as is attested by the Rev. Dr. Pearce in his *Reply to the Defence of the letter to Dr. Waterland* and by Dr. Waterland in his *Scripture Vindicated* and by the several books I have wrote and published, a list wherof is here unto annexed, will your Honour to some pity and compassion that I may not rot and miserably perish in this loathsome tayl[?] for the sake of so small a matter as fifty shillings. And the Almighty will infinitely reward your Honour for the same. And if it be your Honour's pleasure and goodness to contribute towards my enlargement I will acknowledge the same as long as I have Being with the utmost gratitude. I am with the utmost respect your Honour's most faithful most dutiful and devoted humble Servant Moses Marcus.[10]

Marcus mentions his confinement of sixteen months, which would mean, if this were accurate, that he had been continuously locked up in prison since April 1736, some three months before Perceval had allegedly freed him of his debt. Perhaps he had been in prison on and off during that prolonged period, since in the first instance, he was imprisoned for debts stemming from printing fees, and in the second instance, for debts incurred by his wife. In any case, his description of his deteriorating physical condition is pitiful, a stark contrast to his youthful years of wealth and comfort and a rather disheartening predicament for a still young man who had only reached his thirty-sixth year.

Marcus confirms the fact already mentioned by Perceval that he could teach several languages other than Hebrew and Aramaic, which by this time included French, German, Latin, and Italian. He also points out how he filled in for the chief interpreter of the king and was handsomely rewarded. Nevertheless, his clientele, from the list he supplies, are mostly clergymen of varying political allegiances, and it is apparent that their common interest in him is primarily because of his Hebrew skills. He first mentions "his Grace the Duke of Mountague."[11] Next is John Perceval, "the Earl of Egmont," whose presence in the list provides confirmation that indeed these contacts were real ones. Next is Edmund Gibson (1669–1748), the bishop of London, a major figure in the religious and intellectual life of the city. Gibson was known as an Anglo-Saxonist, an antiquarian, a canonist, a writer on popular piety, an administrator, and the most influential of the Georgian prelates.[12] Benjamin Hoadley (1676–1761) was then the bishop of Winchester, a post he had assumed only three years earlier. Hoadley was well known as an outspoken and sometimes controversial leader of the church whose unorthodox views often upset his Anglican colleagues such as William Wake, Daniel Waterland, and Gibson. He was a friend of Samuel Clarke and was alleged to have Arian and deist views.[13] Edward Chandler (1688?–1750), the bishop of Litchfield and Coventry, was a highly significant theologian and philological scholar, a friend of William Wake and Edmond Gibson, and the author of an important defense of Christianity written in response to Anthony Collins, which I shall consider in the next chapter.[14]

Marcus had every reason to take pride in forging relationships with this powerful group of individuals, several of whom were keenly interested in biblical and Hebraic studies. He drew special attention to himself by what he called his confutations of the objections of free thinkers and infidels on behalf of Dr. Daniel Waterland and his associate Zachary Pearce. I will have occasion to discuss these men and his involvement with them later in this chapter. What is important to stress here is that both men acknowledged Marcus's activity on their behalf in their own writings as Marcus specifically mentions. These testimonies, together with that of John Perceval, do much to validate the claims of the entire letter. They suggest that all of these contacts were real, that indeed Moses Marcus knew important people, whether intimately or not, and that regardless of the quality of the relationships he had built, he had succeeded nevertheless in making a name for himself as a Jewish expert of sorts among a highly respected group of Christian clerics. In providing a roadmap of Moses Marcus's acquaintances, the letter offers a unique focus on biblical and Judaic studies through which to assess the common theological and intellectual concerns that led each of these Christian men to seek out this former Jew. When one adds to this mix other theologians such as Wilkins, Wake, and several more to be discussed in later chapters with whom Marcus was also involved, one is confronted with the irony that so marginal an intellectual figure as Moses Marcus, and one who quickly lost his economic standing, was in some respects quite centrally located within a highly influential community of learned clergymen and church officials.

Appended to the letter are two lists, one of books already published by Moses Marcus and a list of his works in press. The four books in the first list include his *Principal Motives*; his *Defence of the Hebrew Bible against Mr. Whiston's Essay,* which is packaged in such a way to obscure the fact that it is not an original work but a translation of Carpzov's criticism; *An Answer to the Letter to Dr. Waterland on the Point of Circumcision,* which is really a learned note, not a full book; and a work he calls here *The Traditions of the Jews with the Expositions of the Talmud,* in two volumes. With regard to the last work, he probably meant his *Ceremonies of the Present Jews,* published first in 1728, although it is a much more modest work, comprising only one slim volume, not two. Among the works in press are his liturgical translations discussed in the previous chapter; a composition called *The Ancient and Modern Customs of the Jews at their Feasts and Fasts*; and *Perke Aboth, Or the Moral and Philosophical Sayings of the Ancient Sages about Three Hundred Years Before Christ.* None of the books in the second list appear to be extant.[15] We might add here that he composed at least one additional work, and possibly a second, both still in manuscript. The first is a small composition called *A Sceme whereby any Person of the meanest Capacity may in a very short time perfect himself in the Hebrew Language without the Assistance of a Master.* It is signed by Moses Marcus but bears no date.[16] The second is called *A Hebrew Grammar by Way of Dialogue.* It is dated July 16, 1750, which would be the only evidence that Marcus was still alive at mid-century, but it is signed as "Mark. Moses, Teacher in Oxford," who is most likely a different author.[17]

Whatever his ultimate aims in composing each of these works, especially the comprehensive surveys of Jewish praxis and literature—either to build a reputation, or to present a favorable image of Judaism, or simply to make money—Moses Marcus's ultimate accomplishment, had he actually produced all of these works, would have been to provide important rudimentary guides of the Jewish faith, its ethics, and its ritual life to a readership of uninformed Christians and Jews alike. Of course, similar guides and broad histories of Judaism composed by Jewish and Christian writers were already available in English translation in his time; consider, for example, those of Modena, Buxtorf, Basnage, and even Prideaux. And by the end of the century the prolific Jewish publisher and translator David Levi had actually completed a life-long project similar in many respects to what Moses Marcus the convert had planned some sixty years earlier.[18]

Marcus's first publication following *The Principal Motives* was his *The Ceremonies of the Present Jews,* which was published in two essentially identical editions in London in 1728 and 1729. The author's name is not affixed to either volume, although Cecil Roth and several other cataloguers have assumed that Marcus was indeed the author. In light of his confirmation in his letter to Sloane that he had prepared a volume of a similar nature, I have no reason to doubt this identification. His later publication on behalf of Dr. Waterland similarly omits his name, a choice, in either case, probably of the publisher, not the author, who certainly took great pride in his publications, as his letter to Sloane indicates. The full title offers an overview of this modest volume: *The Ceremonies . . . Being a Short and Succinct Account of the Meats that are clean and unclean to them. Their Manner of Killing. Their praying at Synagogue, and at Home. Their Washing and Bathing themselves. Their Marriage Ceremonies. Divorce. Precepts of the Women. Of Circumcision. Their Proselytes. Synagogues. Schools. Learning. Contracts. Witnesses. Oaths. Vows. Sickness. Death. Burial. Mourning. Prayers for the Dead. Belief of Resurrection. Paradise. Purgatory. Hell. Of their Priests and Rabbins. Their Manner of keeping the Sabbath. Passover. The Tabernacles. And all others their Feasts and Fasts. To which are added, The Thirteen Articles of their Faith, and an Account of the Sects of the Jews, the Phariseans, Sadduceans, and Esseniens; the Samaritans, Caraites, and Rabbinists.*

The preface of the volume offers little justification for its publication other than the fact that while others have written more voluminous works on the subject, the virtue of this volume is its brevity as "it appears under the trifling Form of a Pamphlet."[19] One might ask initially why Marcus decided to compose this work in the first place. Having repudiated his own heritage, having waged war on the rabbinic tradition and its chief representative in London, David Nieto, why was he engaged in presenting an ostensibly objective portrait of Jewish ceremonial life that he had previously found so reprehensible? Moreover, this was a project primarily concerned not with ancient Judaism but with contemporary Jews, a kind of ethnography of their actual beliefs and practices. Why was he particularly interested in highlighting this living community, and who were the readers his publisher had in mind who would be interested in reading such a portrayal? A conclusive answer to any of these questions is not easily forthcoming based on the scanty information the volume presents, but a careful look at a part of the preface to the volume might at least offer a deeper sense of Marcus's conflicted objectives in compiling this manual.

Marcus opens with a definition of the Jewish religion as one consisting of "three articles": laws, ceremonies, and customs, which in turn derive from three different "Originals," the written law, the oral law, and customs. He defines the written law as those precepts contained in the Pentateuch while the oral law "is a Collection of the Explanations that have been made by their Rabbins or Doctors, upon the Written Law, at different Times, in after Ages." The customs are such practices "as have been introduc'd at sundry Times and Places." He then offers an example to illustrate the distinctions he is making. The written law forbids Jews from working while the oral law spells out thirty-nine categories of prohibited work. With regard to a Sabbath custom, "some scrupulous Persons . . . say, that carrying a Handkerchief in ones Pocket is forbidden by Virtue of that precept; which last is an Example of a Custom."[20]

This utterly simple explanation is followed by the blanket statement that for the Jews there is no essential difference between the written law and the oral law; what vary considerably are the customs, "particularly the Spanish or Portuguese, and Germans, betwixt whom there is almost as great an Animosity as betwixt Calvinists and Lutherans." He emphasizes that the chief difference between the groups concerns liturgy and religious rites and leads to their even building separate synagogues in which to pray. The German and Polish Jews "are more preciser than the Portuguese, in observing a great Number of trifling Ceremonies." At the same time, the Spanish and Portuguese "claim the Preeminence" both because their kings derived from the tribe of Judah and because they expect the Messiah "to be born of them." Accordingly, they do not intermarry with the Germans.[21]

Marcus then offers several learned speculations on the origin of these ceremonies, proposing that they emerged as a distinguishing mark among the nations, or as the remnants of Egyptian worship to which the multitudes were once exposed. He also distinguishes between the view of "our Divines," who "take great Pains to make all the Ceremonies of the five Books of Moses appear mystical to us, with relation to the New Testament," and "the Naturalists," who reduce the meaning of these ceremonies to physical explanations such as climate or disease. But, as he puts it, however we Christians frame any answer to the question, the Jews themselves think otherwise. Because of their stress on ritual worship, they neglect the essential part of their religion, "and at last became by Superstition and prejudice, the nursing Mother of Ignorance, to be meer Hypocrites, for which their Prophets and Christ's Apostles, very severely reproved them, but to no Purpose. They obstinately persisted in their ways, and that Spirit has run in the Veins of that Nation through all Ages."[22]

When the Jews were dispersed, the rabbis compiled the laws into two books, the Mishnah and the Talmud, whose sheer bulks far exceed the Bible itself. Furthermore,

they vended them under the specious Title of mosaical Traditions, although the greatest Part of them had no other Foundation, than the Ambition of having their particular Decisions and Whimsies, (of which the *Talmud* is full) to pass for Oracles pronounced upon the Mount Sinai. Since that time their Successors have commented again upon those Books, and enjoined their Explanations as precepts to be observed, under the Title of Customs: So that the Laws, Ceremonies, and Customs of the Jews, are swelled to an incredible Number, and increase daily; and it is to be feared that their superstitious Ceremonies, like Weeds, out-grow, and over-shade, and at last quite stifle the Morality intended by the Written Law.[23]

I have presented this part of Marcus's explication of Jewish ceremonies to illustrate the mixed messages he offers his readers in this seemingly simple but, in fact, highly complex presentation of his former lifestyle and culture, and his former self. To the reader of his previous work, the last passages have a familiar ring as he excoriates the rabbis and their overgrown legal weeds, which stifle the morality of the original core of Judaism. But what about the first part, presenting Judaism in a relatively objective and fair manner, as the Jews might have seen it themselves, offering, along the way, various theories regarding the origins of the ceremonies presented dispassionately and straightforwardly? And why write a book that summarizes Jewish ceremonies and customs in a compact but relatively objective manner if the ultimate object is to disparage and undermine the entire edifice of rabbinic Judaism in the first place? I confess that there is no clear answer except to contextualize Marcus's inner conflict as one typical of other converts who similarly published compendia of Jewish ceremonies for Christian readers.[24] Were they simply exploiting their previous knowledge for monetary reasons, or was there something deeper driving them to present their former lives in a truthful manner, albeit allowing for occasional outbursts of hostility to legitimate their newly established Christian selves? It strikes me that with the exception of the passages quoted above, Marcus is generally restrained in his presentation of Judaism throughout the volume. In a later section, he explains the Talmud without any negative characterization at all.[25] Perhaps this is so because of his ongoing ambivalence to the Judaism he had abandoned. It also might have something to do with the scholarly standards expected of him by his readers or even those he set for himself. If indeed he proposed to present a summary of Jewish practice, he was required to offer a fair appraisal to the best of his ability. Whatever the ultimate reason that motivated him to write this "trifling form of a pamphlet," it clearly established a pattern more or less consistent with his subsequent publications: that the same person who had abandoned Judaism for the spiritual ideals he discovered in Christianity had paradoxically also become Judaism's faithful expositor and interpreter.

During the same period in which Marcus published his work on the Jewish ceremonies, he saw two of his other works brought to press: his translation of Carpzov's critique of William Whiston in 1729, and a defense of Daniel Waterland against his outspoken critic Conyers Middleton in 1731. These publications placed Marcus at the center of two major controversies about the authenticity of the Hebrew text of the Bible among Christian clergy of differing theological perspectives. It was by virtue of these two relatively modest works that he gained a reputation not only as a defender of the Hebrew text as transmitted by the Jewish tradition, but also as an ally of the orthodox theologians in their fight with Arians,

Latitudinarians, and deists. I consider Marcus's work on Whiston in the next chapter while I focus on Marcus's support of Waterland in the remainder of this one.

Daniel Waterland (1683–1740) was a leading clerical official at Cambridge, where he built a reputation as a major apologist for Christian orthodoxy, defending Trinitarian Christianity against the Arianism promoted by Samuel Clarke and his followers at the university. Clarke attacked Waterland for relying too heavily on the testimony of the church fathers and on tradition to make his case on behalf of the Trinity. Waterland indeed preferred history and theological inquiry over a direct and personal approach to Scripture. He also rejected Clarke's Newtonian synthesis made famous in the Boyle lectures. For Waterland, orthodoxy required the acceptance of the priority of Scripture and the injunctions of faith over the merely intellectual claims of mathematical demonstrations.

Having established himself as the leading defender of the orthodox doctrine of the Trinity, he turned his attention to the deists in a book entitled *Scripture Vindicated,* which was published in 1730–32 in three volumes. Here he attacked Matthew Tindal's *Christianity as Old as the Creation* by claiming that Scripture was often written in a parabolic or metaphoric manner and could not be simply dismissed on the basis of a superficial literal reading. Scripture also revealed an authentic historical record as well as the essential doctrines of Christian faith unavailable to natural religion alone.[26]

A year later, Conyers Middleton (1683–1750) responded to Waterland's book in his *A Letter to Dr. Waterland Containing Some Remarks on his Vindication of Scripture.* Middleton was a highly nonconventional and polemical writer who had earlier published a work arguing that the rituals of the Roman Catholic Church derived from pagan religion. His argument against Waterland was not to defend the deists but to argue that Waterland's approach in proving the historical accuracy of every biblical statement was flawed from the start. Instead, the Christian theologian should invest his energy in defending a traditional religion and to confute the ungrounded assumptions of a so-called religion of nature. Religion was invented, Middleton claimed, to compensate for the insufficiency of reason.[27]

Middleton's crude formulations provoked further response from the Anglican high churchmen allied with Waterland. Zachary Pearce (1690–1774), a former student of William Wake and later the bishop of Rochester, immediately rose to Waterland's defense in his *A Reply to the Letter to Dr. Waterland,* published in the same year. He deplored Middleton's attempt to undermine the historical accuracy of the biblical text in which he showed great irreverence to Moses as well as Waterland. The pamphlet war between the two continued as Middleton responded to Pearce in 1732 and Pearce published his final rejoinder in the same year. In the end, other high churchman joined the ruckus, and Middleton, unrepentant to the end, saw his reputation tarnished by the accusation of infidelity to the Christian faith.[28]

Moses Marcus's role in this clash between the defenders of orthodoxy and their outspoken critic was limited to discussing one factual error among the plethora of accusations Middleton had made impugning the historical accuracy of the Bible. Yet despite the circumscribed nature of his attack on Middleton, given his thorough knowledge of the sources, Marcus was able to raise doubts regarding Middleton's scholarly abilities as a biblical critic. In coming to the defense of Waterland's traditional reading of the text, Marcus seems to have pleased both Waterland and Pearce, as they both acknowledged, and this in turn was a source of great pride to the young convert, as is evident in his letter to Hans Sloane, reproduced earlier in this chapter.

The specific issue in the debate between Waterland, Middleton, and Pearce that caught Marcus's attention revolved around the commandment of circumcision as described in Genesis 17. Waterland, in his *Scripture Vindicated,* had refuted Tindal's contention that the ceremony derived from Egyptian practice. Challenging Tindal's unreliable sources, Waterland simply defended circumcision because God had demanded it: "It is plain that Abraham submitted to it in Obedience only to a divine Command, and he received it as a Sign and Seal of the Covenant of Grace between God and him." He ignored Tindal's accusations that it was dangerous or wrong, and instead accused him of presuming to know God's ways, which is blasphemy.[29]

Middleton's primary critique of Waterland's discussion of circumcision was focused on the question of how a religious duty could involve so much pain and danger. Citing John Spenser (1630–93) and John Lightfoot (1602–95), who had quoted Maimonides, Middleton maintained that Maimonides and the rabbis of the Talmud had also expressed concern for the hazards involved in the cutting and had even prohibited it if actual risk of life was involved. Middleton, citing Lightfoot, even maintained that a standing law existed among the rabbis excusing a person from circumcising a son if he had already lost three children from the operation.[30]

Zachary Pearce was the first to reply to Middleton's allegations, accusing him of mistranslating Maimonides into English and for citing Dr. Spenser carelessly. He noted that Middleton had omitted the word "sometimes" in Spenser's account, which considerably mitigated the import of his statement. Circumcision was not *always* hazardous; it was only *sometimes* so. Pearce furthermore dismissed the notion of a standing law excusing a fourth son from the operation if three previous ones had died as a result of the operation. Lightfoot had not mentioned such a law nor was there frequent mortality owing to circumcision.[31]

It was at this point in the debate that Moses Marcus published his pamphlet, which was entitled: *An Answer to the Letter to Dr. Waterland; in relation to the Point of Circumcision, wherein the Letter-Writer's gross mistakes are examin'd and confuted.* Marcus's name does not appear on the composition but, as we have seen, he explicitly mentions this work in his list of his publications to Hans Sloane, and Daniel Waterland acknowledged that Marcus indeed was the author. His primary contribution to this discussion was to cite the original texts upon which Spenser and Lightfoot had relied. In so doing, he was quite willing to embarrass his opponent for not meeting the scholarly standards necessary to use these texts. He writes:

I will endeavor to convince you (if truth and reason will do it) of your mistakes on that subject, owing perhaps to haste, or to your having had but very slender Acquaintance with what concerns the Jewish Talmuds and Traditions . . .Yet you make no scruple of taking upon Truth, the stories contain'd in Lightfoot . . . and Spenser . . . ; not searching the Originals, which, if look'd into, might have prevented your Misconceptions. . . . I am apt to believe, you are not much acquainted with the Hebrew language. . . . How then can you pretend to be a proper judge in an Affair of such great Importance?[32]

Marcus then cites Maimonides in the original, indicating that there was no rabbinic standing law suspending the ceremony if three children were killed. He utilizes a range of other rabbinic sources to indicate the fact that there were no risks involved. He is surprised how Lightfoot could make such a gross mistake in reading Hebrew sources and he is offended by Middleton's unsubstantiated claims based on a lack of knowledge: "How can you talk so rashly on a subject you were not acquainted with, not understanding the nature of Talmudic Disputations?" For Marcus, as it was for Daniel Waterland, "circumcision was instituted out of the great love of God to Abraham and his seed which was for a sign in his Covenant with them." Marcus adds, "I have made it my Business to enquire among the Jews, whether any person or child ever died of the Operation . . . Yea, many have come from Spain and Portugal and have been circumcised at the age of sixty, seventy, and have never died of it." He referred, of course, to members of the community of former *conversos* in London and Amsterdam who had returned to Judaism as adults and had undergone adult circumcision.[33]

Marcus had most effectively undermined Middleton's entire argument and his use of sources. Here was his opportunity then, in closing, to link his position directly with that of Dr. Waterland and to position himself as a defender of the cleric's honor: "For you have prov'd nothing, and have taken the Liberty to abuse Dr. Waterland . . . in a most ungentlemanlike manner, upon false Grounds and unsupported Evidences, poring in the Dark, talking you knew not what, and censuring you knew not why."[34]

In the meantime, Middleton had again published a response to Pearce. Either he did not notice Moses Marcus's attack on him or he chose to ignore it. In his reply, he cites in full the passages in Spenser and Lightfoot. According to the Spenser text, Middleton claimed, Maimonides had said that circumcision was indeed "res durissima et difficillima," and Lightfoot was the source of the rabbinic standing rule regarding a fourth child. He reiterates his general stance that he was not attacking Christianity or Waterland but the latter's ineffectual approach to fighting deism.[35]

It was left to Pearce to have the final word. In his pamphlet of 1732, Pearce gives due credit to Moses Marcus by citing his words directly: "But what is more at this time of day you might have known from a Pamphlet, intitled, An Answer to your Letter on the Point of Circumcision that Spenser or rather Buxtorf, whom he followed had quite mistaken the sense of Maimonides in this passage. I differ not much from the aforementioned Gentleman [He had called him earlier simply, 'the Answerer']."[36] Waterland too had not failed to notice Moses Marcus's contribution to his debate. In fact, Waterland had previously cited Marcus's earlier translation of Carpzov in his *Scripture Vindicated,* referring to it generously as "Moses Marcus's Defence of the Hebrew Text, Against Mr. Whiston."[37] Now in a personal letter to Pearce, reacting to Pearce's second reply to Middleton and to another work by a Mr. Chapman, Waterland writes, "I could have wished also that you had made some reference to Mr. Chapman's piece on the Languages, as you have done to Moses Marcus on Circumcision."[38] This time, at least in private correspondence, the lowly convert who had boldly and effectively defended the powerful church leader and the sanctity of the biblical text from the spurious accusations of an uninformed dabbler in Hebrew sources, had received his due recognition. He had been mentioned by name!

Chapter 4

Restoring the "True Text" of the Old Testament: William Whiston and His Critics, Johann Carpzov and Moses Marcus

In 1722 William Whiston (1667–1752), the enthusiastic but eccentric advocate and popularizer of Newtonian cosmology and the author of numerous works on mathematics, physics, and astronomy, published a book entitled *Essay Towards Restoring the True Text of the Old Testament and for Vindicating the Citations made thence in the New Testament.* Within a very short time, the work triggered an enormous storm of controversy throughout England and even beyond. Like Newton himself, Whiston had consistently been drawn to prophecy and biblical studies, and he devoted considerable effort to the study of the biblical text and the history of ancient Judaism and of the church, as well as chronology, liturgy, miracles, and demonology. He had also devoted himself to translating the works of the ancient Jewish historian Josephus into English, a translation that would be published and republished for centuries. His vast learning, however, never tempered the idiosyncratic and controversial nature of many of his theological and scriptural positions. Like Samuel Clarke, his close associate, he was accused of Arianism by his more orthodox Anglican colleagues, was expelled from Cambridge, and even endured heresy proceedings against him, which were eventually dropped.[1]

Whiston's basic position with regard to biblical prophecy had long been evolving prior to 1722. As early as 1707, he presented the core of his argument within the framework of the distinguished Robert Boyle lectures and then published them a year later in a book called *The Accomplishment of Scripture Prophecies.* From the outset, Whiston emphasized how critical the study of prophecy was in demonstrating the Christian faith because of the inadequacy of the design argument in convincing deists and unbelievers that God existed and actively intervened in the world. Employing the methods of an experimental scientist, he claimed that the more proofs of prophecy he could muster from the Bible and even extra-biblical works such as the Sibylline Oracles, the more solid the foundations of Christianity would become. There was simply strength in numbers. His system of prophetic hermeneutics could only work, however, if each prophecy he identified had only one fulfillment, and that was in Jesus Christ: "I observe that the Stile and Language of the Prophets, as it is often peculiar and enigmatical, so it is always single and determinate, and not capable of those double Intentions, and typical Interpretations, which most of our late Christian Expositors are so full of upon all Occasions . . . for that can by no other method so well attempted as by the Demonstration, that all their old Predictions, relating to the Messias, whose periods are already past, have been properly and literally, without any recourse to Typical, Foreign, and Mystical Expositions fulfill'd in Jesus of Nazareth, our Blessed Lord and Savior."[2]

Whiston knew well that his insistence on a literal understanding of prophetic fulfillment without recourse to allegorical interpretations or to the possibility that prophecies might apply simultaneously to more than one object was controversial and went against the grain of generations of Christian exegesis. But upholding this one to one correspondence between the Old Testament prophecy and its outcome in Christian teaching was the only way in which the validity of Christianity could be upheld: "If the double intention in Prophecies be allow'd by us Christians, as to those Predictions which were to be fulfilled in our Savior Christ; and if we own that we can no otherwise shew their completion, then by applying them secondarily and typically to our Lord, after they had in their first and primary intention been already plainly fulfill'd in the times of the Old Testament: We lose all the real advantage of these ancient Prophecies, as to the proof of our common Christianity; and besides expose ourselves to the insults of Jews and Infidels in our Discourses with them."[3] Whiston illustrated the absurdity of allowing a prophecy to apply to more than one thing at a time. If, for example, Isaiah 53 applied both to Hezekiah and to Jesus, "could we suppose that any Jew or Infidel of a competent Judgment, would be persuaded that our Jesus was the true Messias, and Son of God. . . ?"[4]

Several years later in a retort to two of his critics, who still upheld that it was possible to allow prophecy to stand for more than one object, he clarified even more precisely the scientific model on which his position was based: "And I verily believe, that till the learned Christian imitate the learned Philosophers and Astronomers of the present Age, who have almost entirely left off Hypotheses and Metaphysicks, for Experiments and Mathematicks; I mean till they be content to take all things, that naturally depend, thereon, from real Facts, and original Records; without the Byass of Hypothesis, or Party, or Inclination; then I say I verily believe that Disputes and Doubts, Scepticism and Infidelity will increase upon us. . . ." And later he adds: "And if once the Learned come to be as wise in religious Matters, as they are now generally become in those that are Philosophical and Medical, and Juridical; if they will imitate the Royal

Society, the College of Physicians, or the Judges in Courts of Justice . . .
I verily believe that the Variety of Opinions . . . will gradually diminish;
the Objections against the Bible will greatly wear off, and genuine Christianity . . . will more and more take Place among Mankind."[5]

The problem Whiston soon discovered was that finding a one-to-one
correspondence between prophetic statements in the Old Testament and
their fulfillment in the New was not as easy as it appeared. Some prophecies could not easily be interpreted to apply exclusively to Jesus. If indeed
his allegedly scientific project of Christian prophetic hermeneutics could
not be properly carried out, all Christian claims of divine truth might be
called into question. There was accordingly only one conceivable way of
explaining the gap between the two testaments: the original Hebrew text
had been corrupted. This was the inevitable conclusion Whiston reached
in his publication of 1722. Since the present Hebrew copies of the Old
Testament do not quite correspond to the texts "cited by our Saviour, his
Apostles, and the rest of the Writers of the New Testament, out of the
Old," it stands to reason that over the course of the years the present version of the Hebrew Bible was altered and the culprits in this falsification
were none other than the Jews: "The Jews, about the beginning of the Second Century of the Gospel, greatly alter'd and corrupted their Hebrew
and Greek Copies of the Old Testament; and that in many places, on purpose, out of Opposition to Christianity."[6]

The argument thus framed was a frontal attack against the Jews for
consciously and purposefully corrupting their own sacred text. They took
this radical step because "they had therefore no other possible Way of
stopping the farther Progress of the Gospel among them, in their own
Power, but this, of altering and corrupting their own Copies." Since Christians subsequently did not study the Hebrew language, and "that, by Consequence, the original Sacred Books were alone in the Jewish Hands,"
Christians were easily deceived.[7]

Whiston insisted that his argument was legitimated by the remarkable
strides in the study of the extra-biblical literature of antiquity now being
edited and published in his day, including the Samaritan Pentateuch, the
Apostolic Constitutions, the Greek Psalms, and especially the work of
Josephus, all of which provided alternative readings of the Hebrew text
of the Bible. Some forty years prior to the ambitious project of Benjamin
Kennicott and Robert Lowth to create a Christian version of the Hebrew
Bible, Whiston was already calling for a similar initiative whereby "a
great search should be made in all Parts of the World for Hebrew Copies,
that have never come into the hands of the Masorets."[8]

Almost from the moment that Whiston's book appeared, his critics
were lining up to challenge his highly controversial conclusions. This ris-
ing tide of opposition appeared to make Whiston more defiant and ready

to take on each and every one of his detractors. A year later he published a supplement to the book, arguing that "the Canticles is not a sacred book of the Old Testament" and was never considered as such either by Jews or Christians.[9] In 1724, the stakes were raised considerably when the freethinker Anthony Collins entered the public arena with a scathing attack against Whiston. Whiston was obliged to publish a whole series of successive publications responding to Collins and his other critics; these in turn provoked more critical replies from the pen of Collins during the next several years. Collins's work, in turn, generated its own critical outcry, especially from those clerics who were incensed that such an outspoken critic of traditional Christianity would dare to present himself as a legitimate defender of the Christian faith.

In the course of this raging and protracted controversy over Whiston's provocative arguments and Collins's counterarguments regarding the biblical text, Moses Marcus elected to enter the battle with the publication of what might be deemed his most important scholarly contribution. The full title of Moses Marcus's work published in London in 1729 reads *A Defence of the Hebrew Bible In Answer to the Charge of Corruption Brought Against it by Mr. Whiston in His Essay towards restoring the true Text of the Old Testament, where Mr. Whiston's Pretences are particularly Examined and Confuted, by the Reverend Dr. Carpzov of Leipsick, translated from the Latin, with Additional Notes by Moses Marcus, A Converted Jew, and Teacher of the Oriental Language.* The long-winded description of the work does underscore the relatively modest role of Marcus as translator and annotator. Nevertheless, unlike several of his previous works, his name is prominently displayed on the title page, providing a kind of self-presentation, flagging his credentials as a teacher of Oriental languages, not modern European languages or Latin this time, and defining himself as "a converted Jew." The latter designation elicits a number of questions. Why was it necessary or important for Marcus to identify himself as a convert in the first place? Was this his publisher's decision or his own? Did the fact that he was a former Jew perhaps lend more credence to the translator and his Hebraic credentials? And why the designation "converted Jew" rather than "Jewish convert" or "Jewish convert to Christianity"? Was this a mere convention or does the term "converted Jew" not place the emphasis on Moses Marcus's still Jewish status? That is, although he had converted, might he still be perceived as a Jew in some sense?

Whatever the answers to these questions, it is obvious that Marcus was proud of this book, and he had good reason to feel that way. Although his accomplishment was no more than a mere translation and annotation of the work of a highly respected German scholar, and it appeared relatively late, at the tail end of the debate over Whiston, nevertheless, it placed him very close to the center of a highly significant conversation among Christian theologians, church leaders, and their free-thinking critics that challenged and stimulated English society for well over a decade. The sheer number of pamphlets elicited by Whiston's work and that of his chief critic, Anthony Collins, is staggering. It indicates that the highly charged controversy had touched a most sensitive nerve of many clergy and lay writers alike because, on the most fundamental level, it challenged the very claims of the New Testament and the Church to speak the truth, to claim that it was actually conveying the divine revelation. Marcus's decision to enter this public debate was surely calculated on his part. Perhaps he was in fact claiming that as "a converted Jew' he had the authority to add his considerable weight to a discussion that touched the very core of Christian identity.

A thorough look at Marcus's project is both revealing for what it accomplishes and for what it does not accomplish. In publishing this work, Marcus understood quite well that the public forum surrounding Whiston was a perfect vehicle for displaying his own skills as translator and expositor of the Hebrew Bible. Ironically, the book also explicitly reveals his severe limitations as an exegete of rabbinic literature. His own sense of how to respond to Whiston was relatively unoriginal and unimaginative, relying almost exclusively on the insights of the scholarly Carpzov. While Marcus was obviously aware of the provocative arguments of Collins against Whiston, which Carpzov had also noticed but had chosen to ignore, Marcus remained conspicuously silent about their implications for the study of the Bible and rabbinic literature by Christians. Having reached the apex of his literary career in translating a learned German expositor of the Hebrew Bible on a burning issue of his day, he ultimately proved incapable of comprehending the real import of this controversy for Christian self-understanding. Ultimately, that role would be left to others.

Johann Gottlob Carpzov (1679–1767), a professor of Oriental languages at Leipzig and a theologian, was a well-respected Hebraist with a wide-ranging knowledge of Jewish sources. His sweeping introduction to the Old Testament, the *Critica sacra*, was published in three volumes in 1728 in Latin. Only the third volume constituted his reply to Whiston and was the text Moses Marcus selected for his English translation. That Carpzov had not only noticed Whiston's publication but had chosen to respond to it in a three-hundred-page critique appended to his biblical commentary offers significant testimony to the threat Whiston had posed to Christian thinkers far beyond the clerical circles of London. Carpzov continued to publish throughout his own life, including his annotations to Goodwin's *Moses and Aaron*, along with a special appendix with the title "The Synagogue Treated with Honor," which was his own take on Christianity's debt to ancient Jewish customs.[10]

Marcus had good reason to appreciate Carpzov's fine qualities as a scholar and his commitment to the integrity of the Hebrew Scripture. He pays him the highest compliment in his introduction, acknowledging that he had been in Leipzig and met him on several occasions: "The very Reverend and Worthy Author, I have had the Honour to see, more than once at Leipsick, being Professor of Divinity in that famous University and Archdeacon of the Church. And I have often heard him spoken of in Germany in terms of very great Respect, as of another Buxtorf." He then lists Carpzov's learned publications of the Old Testament and pays them high compliment. He finally singles out Carpzov's treatise on Whiston, which Marcus considers "an Answer not only to Whiston, but to other very considerable Men, [Stephanus] Morinus, [Louis] Cappellus, [Isaac] Vossius, [Richard] Simon, [Paul] Pezron, and [Jean] Le Clerc from whom Mr. Whiston in a Manner has barely copied."[11] In making Carpzov available to the English reader, Marcus pointed to his own still-intimate ties to Germany as well as to his familiarity with Latin scholarship composed by Christian scholars on the Continent.

What immediately follows is one of Marcus's most telling descriptions of himself and his relationship to Judaism and Christianity. In answering his own question regarding why he was inclined to take on this project in the first place, he openly declares:

If any Man be curious enough to ask, why I in particular, have engaged in this Affair, and taken this Part upon Me; it might be sufficient to say, because no body has done it, and I knew not whether any would. But I must further own, that I had a particular Ambition to vindicate the Jews, my own Brethren and Countrymen, from so heavy and heinous a Charge, as that of maliciously and sacrilegiously corrupting and depraving the sacred Text. A hideous Crime, such, as I am confident, They could never have thought of without Horror and Detestation, having been ever most religiously scrupulous in regard to the Sacred Text, and not at all less conscientious in that respect, than even the most pious Christians. Their Infidelity, and Opposition to Christ Jesus my Saviour, (owing to the unconquerable Prejudices of Education) I heartily condemn; And I thank my God, every day of my Life, for giving me a Sight and Sense of my Errors, and bringing me within the Pale of the Christian Church. But still I retain, and ever shall retain that Regard for my Brethren, whom I have left for the Sake of Christ, as to do them all reasonable Justice, and to defend their Reputation against downright Calumny. Such was the Part that Johan. Isaac. A converted Jew, long ago (A.D. 1559) acted against the Papist Lindanus, who had slanderously charged the Jews with corrupting the Hebrew Scriptures, just as Mr. Whiston has done. As he defended his Countrymen, and the Word of God at the same Time, so do I in like Circumstances; but in such a way as I can, not as an Author, but as a humble Translator of another Man's Work, so much better than anything of my own, as being of a very able and first-rate Writer.[12]

Nothing in Marcus's other writing offers so honest an appraisal of his dual loyalties to the religion he had forsaken and to the one he had now embraced as this text does. He is also quite candid in assessing his own limited abilities to translate the work of another author rather than write his own book. He is offended by the notion that Jews are considered corrupters and falsifiers of a text they hold as sacred as the Christians do, and the need to defend their integrity is his overriding consideration in jumping into the debate over Whiston. Whether prophetic statements should be read literally or allegorically, however, is not his concern. Nor is he in a position to offer a response to Whiston's dilemma of how to correlate the prophecies of the New Testament with those of the Old. He is exclusively concerned with defending the reliability of the Hebrew text; on the weightier exegetical issues raised by the Whiston-Collins debate, he is silent. As we shall see, Collins ostensibly embraced a "Jewish" reading of prophecy, a posture with which Marcus might have concurred or at least acknowledged, but here too, he has nothing to say.

What is most revealing is what he does say about modeling his behavior after that of another convert, Johannes Isaac (1515–71), who defended the integrity of the masoretic Hebrew Bible against the charges of the Catholic theologian Wilhelm Lindanus. As Elisheva Carlebach has noted, Moses Marcus's locating of himself in a tradition of converts who defended Jewish interests was not uncommon. He had apparently learned of Johannes Isaac from Carpzov himself, who cited his book against Lindanus. Johannes and his son Stephan, both the subjects of recent studies, underwent multiple conversions from Judaism to Lutheranism to Catholicism and back to Lutheranism. The relations between father and son were strained by the machinations of the Jesuits, who sought to use them for their own purposes. Johannes especially was a prolific author of books on Hebrew and Judaic subjects, in addition to his defense of the biblical text, and was deemed worthy of a professorship in Hebrew studies in Cologne. Nevertheless, both Johannes and his son were consistently accused of insincerity and inconstancy in their profession of the Christian faith. They were Jews who had allegedly become false Christians.[13]

Note that Marcus also labels Johannes "a converted Jew," the label he calls himself, underscoring, as I have intimated, the unique Jewish core of his identity, notwithstanding his conversion. Perhaps we might define Marcus's self-representation, like that of Johannes, in the following way. Marcus saw his affiliation with his former coreligionists primarily in ethnic, intellectual, and social terms rather than in religious ones. Religiously, he was a faithful follower of Jesus Christ. But as he put it, he still felt a strong solidarity with his own "Brethren and Countrymen" and a deep connection to their intellectual and literary legacy. Being "a converted Jew" meant defending the integrity of the transmission of sacred Scripture by Jews and the Jewish exegetical tradition from uninformed critics lacking the proper intellectual and linguistic credentials to understand

Hebrew texts in the first place. Being "a converted Jew" meant staking out a position wherein religious affiliation could be separated from cultural attraction and scholarly commitment.[14]

Marcus appreciates Carpzov primarily because this conservative scholar venerates the biblical text: "He is most averse to that Spirit of Levity, that Wantonness of Criticizing, which pushes Men on to play with holy Things, to tamper needlessly with Texts, whose Reading are already fix'd, and to be hammering out endless Emendations." And he adds: "It is a very easy Matter to fall to hacking and hewing, upon every slight Occasion; and to cut the knot which one cannot readily unty. . . . If the Objection can be taken off, and the Difficulty solved, without altering the Text, it is much better." He has in mind the radical emendations of Louis Cappellus and Jean le Clerc. In the final analysis, he gracefully concludes: "There are still many things in Scripture, as well as in Nature, which are to be brought to light by Degrees, and may remain as useful Matter for future Inquiries. Our Bible, after all, is a very good Bible, and our Hebrew Text a very pure Text."[15]

In his generally conservative nature, in his identification with similarly inclined clergy who revere the text and defend its incorruptibility, and in his discomfort with those critics who irresponsibly emend and tamper with a text that should not be violated, Moses Marcus again recalls the style of Anglo-Jewry's polemical spokesman David Levi at the end of the century. He too devoted all of his energies to argue for the sanctity of the Masoretic Text; he too poked fun at Protestant critics who recklessly proposed emendations upon emendations, and he too felt most comfortable in the company of conservative clergy, defenders of Trinitarian Christianity. Although Marcus acted out his Jewish loyalties as a Christian, and Levi remained loyal to Jewish orthodoxy throughout his long career, they bear an uncanny resemblance. In fact, they are alike in two additional respects as both learned popularizers and polemicists, and as intelligent spokesmen on behalf of Judaism though hardly original thinkers in their own right.[16]

Carpzov's treatise against Whiston is a highly learned refutation of his position based primarily on scholarly grounds. While he alludes to Whiston's alleged Arian tendencies, he generally avoids personal attack. He is acutely aware of Collins's critique of Whiston but deems it more dangerous than the latter's own work and avoids discussing it altogether. He carefully summarizes Whiston's arguments about the corruption of the present Hebrew text and his propositions to restore the original. Carpzov offers learned notes to reveal Whiston's sources and these are supplemented on occasion by Moses Marcus himself. Just as Marcus had done in his introduction, Carpzov points out how the arguments of Whiston are unoriginal and rely on the previous scholarship of men such as

Benedict Spinoza, Hugo Grotius, Louis Cappellus, and Jean le Clerc.[17] He offers a learned discussion of the extant rabbinic Bibles of Venice and Amsterdam and applauds their high standards of scholarship. He acknowledges the inadequacies of the Masoretic Text but is unwilling to dismiss its general reliability. More problematic to use, in his estimation, are the Greek and Samaritan Bibles. To this, Moses Marcus adds his own challenge in a footnote regarding Whiston's uncritical reliance on the Apostolic Constitutions which he had championed as an alternative to the biblical text. Carpzov similarly discounts the over-reliance of Whiston on targumic readings of the Bible and on Philo's authority. He regularly cites medieval Jewish commentators to which Moses Marcus creatively adds his own learned animadversions.[18]

Most interesting is Carpzov's discussion of the seemingly inaccurate citations of the Old Testament in the New. Rather than conclude on the basis of their irreconcilability that the present version of the Old Testament is corrupt, he cites "a person well versed in Talmudick and Rabbinick Learning, namely Guil. Surenhusius," the primary source for Collins, which I shall have occasion to discuss below. He cites him several times and concludes: "Although the Citations of the New Testament may seem almost opposite and contrary to their Originals, and to the Words of the Places from whence they are quoted, yet if we take a more narrow View of them, they rather give us an Explication, and a Kind of Comment upon the Text of the Old Testament." Furthermore, he adds: "For it is evident that the Holy Ghost did not intend everywhere in the New Testament, to abide by the very Words which were used in the Old, but that sometimes it was contrary to his Design to do it."[19]

Moses Marcus offers no reaction to Carpzov's evocation of Surenhusius or to his explicit criticism of Whiston's excessive literalism in reading New Testament prophecy. He also offers no reaction to Carpzov's genuine appreciation of the Jews and their rabbinic authorities and his spirited approbation of their courage against considerable adversity: "When being expell'd from their own Habitations, stripp'd and depriv'd of their Religion, Polity, Temple, Books, Riches, and sacerdotal Order, they were intent only upon this one thing, that they might in any Degree restore their Religion, so shattered and broken to Pieces, and that they might be more solicitous about preferring their Worship . . . and about transmitting them [their ceremonies] to their Posterity . . . than about a diligent Revising of the Sacred Copies." Elsewhere Carpzov volunteers his accurate knowledge of Babylonian Judaism to counter Whiston again: "Further, such a thing could never have taken effect among the Jews themselves, since the Babylonian Academies and Masters, at that time flourishing in Peace and Plenty, and in the Height of Study and good Literature, would never have suffered a new, false, and adulterated reading to be obtruded upon them, and their own genuine and perfect Copies, which they were then in Possession of, as also their ancient and sacred Character, to be taken away from them, and extorted out of their Hands." Finally, he applauds the integrity of Palestinian Jewry as well, despite its preoccupation with its own security, and singles out "a Man of great Authority among his own People," Rabbi Akiva.[20]

In the end, one senses that Carpzov fully understood the larger issues at stake in the Whiston-Collins debate. His evocation of William Suren-husius and his disagreement with Whiston's view of Christian prophecy suggest that had he wished he could have said much more on these matters. Instead, he focused primarily on the truthfulness of the Hebrew text, on the reliability of its transmission by the rabbis, and on the integrity of the rabbis in not consciously falsifying sacred Scripture.

This caution is even more evident with respect to Moses Marcus. One might argue that as a mere translator of Carpzov's words, Marcus was in no position to address the larger issues Carpzov himself mostly avoided by ignoring Collins's provocative book. But might it be reasonable to draw further implications from Marcus's caution? Perhaps his choice of translating Carpzov in the first place exposed his own intellectual limitations in not composing an original work as well as his own ambivalence about the rabbis and postbiblical Judaism. He had indeed begun his professional life as a Christian expositor of Judaism with a frontal attack on Nieto's defense of the oral law. He had later presented Judaism in more positive terms or at least in neutral ones in his later writings, but a certain vacillation surely remained. What is noticeably absent in his comments on Jews and Judaism is an appreciation of rabbinic exegesis or the legitimacy of the oral law. Instead, he limits himself only to empha-sizing the Jewish fidelity to the Hebrew text of the Old Testament and to vindicating the rabbis as zealous guardians of that text. This is surely the crux of his introduction to his translation of Carpzov's work: to defend the Jews for their faithful transmission of the written law but also to condemn them simultaneously for their infidelity, that is, their belief in an oral law that contradicts and supersedes the truths of Christianity. For him, his stance was identical with that of the convert Johannes Isaac. Exculpating the Jews against the false charges of Whiston was legitimate; assigning value to rabbinic exegesis and legal authority was not. It would become a primary objective of other Christian thinkers to reassess the rabbinic tradition and its relation to ancient Christianity in a way Marcus was incapable of doing or unwilling to do. Their approach to the rabbis became more prominent in England through the writing of Anthony Collins and the storm of reactions his work elicited, to which I now turn.

Chapter 5

Anthony Collins's Attack on William Whiston: Could the Rabbis Ultimately Rescue Christianity from Its Own Exegetical Crisis?

Anthony Collins (1676–1729), the well-known intellectual associated with both John Toland and Matthew Tindal and deeply influenced by John Locke, entered the fray surrounding William Whiston in 1724 when he published *A Discourse of the Grounds and Reasons of the Christian Religion.* Collins called himself a freethinker, by which term he identified a person who impartially uses his understanding to determine the meaning of propositions and to judge their truth or falsity based on available evidence. He argued in his *A Discourse on Free-Thinking,* published in 1713, that free-thinking was a universal right and a duty in deciding religious matters. He pointed out how the clergy differed on almost every issue and called for a rational evaluation of all their utterances.[1]

While he claimed he was a believing Christian, his enemies labeled him a skeptic, a cynic, a deist, even an atheist. Modern scholarship on Collins is similarly divided in trying to assess his true convictions, and these differing evaluations will complicate our attempt to understand his actual position in his critique of Whiston. Whatever controversy he created over his essay on freethinking, the tempest over his *Discourse of the Grounds and Reasons of the Christian Religion* was spectacular, evoking no less than thirty-five responses in print.

After poking fun at Whiston's style of writing, Collins offers a succinct statement of the man's conclusion and its import for the Christian faith: "Mr. Whiston proposes his Sceme of a corrupted Old Testament, as the best and only Method of defending Christianity, which, according to him, had a rational Dependence on the Old Testament before it was corrupted; and that he apprehends, that the Sceme or Supposition of an uncorrupted Old Testament really destroys the Truth of Christianity, and gives the Deists, Jews, and Infidels, a just Subject of Triumph over it, which, according to him, is now in an irreconcileable State with, and depends not on, the present Old Testament."[2]

Collins had certainly understood the logic of Whiston's position correctly. Old Testament prophecies referred to in the New Testament often did not correspond with their originals. These prophecies meaningfully could only refer to one object, which would be an event in the life of Jesus Christ. Furthermore, they could only be understood literally, not figuratively and not allegorically, to have any real meaning. If indeed there was a gap between the two testaments, either Christianity was foundationless and false, or alternatively, the text of the Old Testament was corrupted and unreliable. If we could construct its original text, we would again find full correspondence between the two documents.

But Collins finds the notion that the Old Testament is corrupted absurd and unfounded. Moreover, contrary to Whiston's position, "to suppose the Old Testament so corrupted . . . is to give up Christianity to Jews and Infidels." He continues:

Do not the Jews take it for granted on Vulgar tradition among themselves, that they have a true Copy of the Books of the Old Testament? And do not all Infidels take it for granted upon the vulgar Tradition of Jews and Christians, that the present Books of the Old Testament are the very Books, upon which, not only Jews, but Christians ground their Religion? And will not both Jews and Infidels think the cause of Christianity sufficiently weak, if Christians once allow, that the New Testament depends not on the (present) Old Testament, contrary to what Christians have for many ages past asserted, and to what the primitive Fathers and the Apostles themselves, according to all Appearances, asserted before them?[3]

The Jews had no reason to corrupt the text, as Whiston asserts. If they had, Collins adds, the ancient Christians would have detected their forgeries long ago. Furthermore, even if Whiston were correct that the present text of the Old Testament is false, he would never be able to restore a better text, based on extra-biblical literature such as the works of Philo or Josephus, which are even more unreliable. His conclusion utterly mocks the pretentious effort of Whiston to discover a new Hebrew Bible to replace the present one: "So that I will venture to say that a Bible restor'd, according to Mr. Whiston's Theory, will be a mere Whistonian Bible, a Bible confounding and not containing the true Text of the Old Testament."[4]

Collins had seemingly succeeded in undermining Whiston's entire scheme. If Christianity rested on a scientific method of reading prophecies literally, based on a direct correspondence between the New Testament and the Old, a correspondence that was hopelessly impossible to retrieve, Christians had reached a dead end, or in Collins's words: "For if the Grounds and Reasons for Christianity, contained in the Old Testament, were lost, Christianity was then lost."[5]

The only recourse for saving Christianity was to adopt an allegorical reading of prophecy. There was no reason to believe that when the New Testament cites the Old, it always does so in a literal way. Christianity need not rise and fall on the arbitrary and rigid notions of Whiston's system.

At this point, Collins offers an alternative way of solving the hermeneutical dilemma Christians faced. He relates that he had recently learned of an entirely novel approach proposed by a distinguished professor of Hebrew studies at the University of Amsterdam named William Surenhusius. Surenhusius "has made an ample Discovery to the World of the Rules, by which, the Apostles cite the Old Testament, and argu'd from thence in a Treatise . . . wherein the whole Mystery of the Apostles applying Scripture in a secondary or typical or mystical, or allegorical Sense seems unfolded." Based on the English report by the journalist Michel de la Roche concerning Surenhusius's book, which was published in 1713, Collins relates the following background. Surenhusius met a rabbi in Amsterdam, "well skill'd in the Talmud, the Cabbala, and the allegorical Books of the Jews." This rabbi had once embraced Christianity but had relapsed into Judaism "on account of the Idolatry of the Papists, yet not perfectly disbelieving the Integrity of the New Testament." Surenhusius shared with the rabbi his exegetical predicament of not knowing how to understand the lack of correspondence between the passages cited in the Old Testament and the New. The rabbi, to his surprise, had no difficulty in reconciling these passages based on his intimate knowledge of rabbinic literature and rabbinic modes of reading and citation. By reading the New Testament by the rules and practices of rabbinic writing, the text becomes fully comprehensible, he maintained. Surenhusius was initially reluctant to consider the manner in which the rabbis cited biblical passages until he "saw St. Paul do so too," after which his anger was appeased."[6]

Collins cannot help but offer a note of sarcasm in observing that a rabbi, albeit one open to the truths of Christianity, had apparently offered a solution to Christians on how to read and appreciate their own scriptural tradition. This conference between Surenhusius and the rabbi was analogous, so it seemed, to that between Luther and the devil: "The Rabbin establishes Christianity; and the Devil Protestantism." Collins offers a generous sampling of examples of how the rabbis cited the Bible and how this directly illuminates a similar method of citation employed in the New Testament. The conclusion is thus inescapable: "Christianity is the allegorical sense of the Old Testament, and is not improperly called mystical Judaism." Furthermore, Paul "understood the secret, divine, and spiritual sense of Judaism which the World that interpreted Judaism knew nothing of." He had been educated by Gamliel and even esteemed by some Jews themselves "as a great *Mekubal,* and profoundly skill'd in the sublime sense of the Bible." And St. Luke as well, "being a great Companion of St. Paul, was no doubt instructed by him in the Cabala of the Jews and in the sublime sense of the Old Testament." Collins unabashedly remarks that perhaps the glory of Christianity rests on allegory, not criticism, and that Christianity is ultimately confirmed by rabbinic learning. How ironic is the fact "that the Apostles, who were men of no literature and education, and never spent their time in the schools of the Rabbis should be such eminent masters in allegory or Rabbinical learning, and should be so excellently vers'd in their traditionary Explications of Prophecies."[7]

Months after Collins had published his book, Whiston angrily responded in *The Literal Accomplishment of Scripture Prophecies, being a full Answer to a late Discourse, of the Grounds and Reasons of the Christian Religion.* After restating and updating his list of predictions of the Old Testament concerning the Messiah, "with their literal Completions in Jesus," and reiterating his belief that the present version of the Old Testament, literally understood, does not in any way serve the interests of Christianity, he ridiculed "those Ten (ridiculous) Rules of Interpretation, or Quotation of the Old Testament, suggested to Surenhusius by a late Jewish Rabbi." He asked for actual proof that they were utilized by Jesus and the Apostles. He concluded with a scathing personal attack on his opponent, raising the obvious question of whether he was actually sincere or not: "Notwithstanding his open and profess'd Infidelity, he ventures, in the most publick and solemn Manner, to declare his unfeigned Acknowledgement of the Divine Providence, of the Truth of the Christian Religion, and of the Books of the Holy Scripture, that is possible to be done among Men. . . . This I call gross Immorality, Impious Fraud, and Laycraft."[8]

He is a bit more revealing in a short work he wrote the following year to refute several of his critics who had seriously upheld the idea that the prophecies could in fact apply to more than one object. Whiston attributed what he called this double sense of prophecies to the later Jews and to their opposition to Christianity. It was their way of "avoiding the old Christian Reasonings from the natural, and single, and literal Sense of those Prophecies, as related to the Messiah and to him only. This behavior reflected no more than Jewish knavery, wickedness, and perfidiousness." It is especially regretful, he added, "that such Ways of Exposition should be taken up by Christians from the modern Jews, as were on purpose invented by them against the Christians."[9]

Whiston accordingly could hardly take seriously Collins's proposed solution to the quandary of Christian exegesis based on the methods of Surenhusius. He attacked instead Collins's character and dismissed the idea that the rabbis had anything useful to teach Christians about interpreting their prophecies. Whiston's verdict that Collins was actually committing an "Impious Fraud" in presenting himself as a believer while ridiculing in the grossest way the very foundations of Christianity became eventually a widely held sentiment shared by Collins's most vocal critics. It also seems to have become a view that is strongly supported by several contemporary scholars who study his work.

The standard interpretation of Anthony Collins's thought is by James O'Higgens. O'Higgens describes Collins's broad background, his vast library, and his particular interest in biblical scholarship. He indicates how well acquainted Collins was with the writings of Grotius, Prideaux, Selden, Pezron, le Clerc, Simon, and others, and how he had even acquired for his library three manuscripts of rabbinic and Karaite provenance: the anti-Christian works of Isaac b. Abraham of Troki (1533–94), Saul Levi Morteira (1596?–1660), and Isaac Orobio de Castro (ca. 1617–87).[10] Despite the evidence of so extensive a background and interest in biblical studies and in Jewish polemics with Christianity, O'Higgens assumes, nevertheless, that Collins's use of Surenhusius was a ruse; he had made the Dutch scholar and his project look ridiculous. He later adds: "It is generally agreed that his attempt to apply his rabbinical rules to the New Testament, if not ridiculous, was yet a failure." It is unclear whether he means that it was a failure by the standards of his day, or a failure by contemporary standards. O'Higgens adds that although Collins claimed that Surenhusius had truly defended Christianity beyond what any author ever did before him, the claim is ridiculous. The typological argument was absurd and basically his argument represented no argument at all. Collins's posture was accordingly that of an anti-Christian; although remaining a member of the Church of England, he had effectively demolished the foundation of traditional Christianity.[11]

Despite this devastating critique, O'Higgens still considers Collins a deist. David Berman, in contrast, sees him as a "speculative atheist." Moreover, along with others such as John Toland, Matthew Tindal, and Charles Blount, Collins had mastered thoroughly the art of theological lying. More than merely writing with irony, Collins actually wrote to lie, that is "not merely saying what you do not mean but aiming to deceive by what you say." For Berman, part of Collins's general strategy was to undermine Christianity through the eccentric theories of prominent churchmen and theologians. His argument against Whiston and his use of Surenhusius are cases in point. Since Whiston had established that the New Testament could only base its truth claims on being the literal fulfillment of Old Testament prophecies, Collins had found an easy target by demonstrating that literal fulfillment was impossible. The only alternative was typological fulfillment by Jesus, but "typology is absurd as nearly anything can be fulfilled by its means." Accordingly, Collins is able to prove that Christianity is groundless. While Berman admits that Christianity never explicitly asserted that typological fulfillment is totally absurd, nevertheless, "it is universally agreed that he [Collins] believed and expected his readers to believe that typology was absurd and false."[12]

Pascal Taranto also analyzes the same material pertaining to Collins and more or less agrees with Berman.[13] Henning Graf Reventlow similarly

summarizes the debate, adding only that Collins misunderstood Surenhusius because he had not read him in the original but only through de
la Roche's summary.[14] I shall consider this point below. Stephen Snobelen provides a recent summary as well, without entertaining the possibility that Collins took allegory seriously and without treating Surenhusius
at all.[15]

We are left basically with a scholarly consensus about Collins's real
intentions. Whether Collins was actually an atheist or a deist, no scholar
has considered the possibility that he was sincere in his attempt to offer
a serious alternative to the predicament Whiston had created for Christianity. Having demolished Whiston's system of literal prophecy as the
foundation of Christian belief, he then discovered an oddball named
Surenhusius to demonstrate cynically the futility of an allegorical reading. He would enhance the ludicrousness of his argument by offering a
comical scenario of a great Christian scholar consorting with a suspect
Jewish rabbi, just as Luther had consorted with the devil, supposedly to
resolve the critical problem of Christian exegesis. The allegorical solution was not only ineffectual; it was tainted by its "mystical," "cabbalist,"
and Jewish origins. In trying to assert their own independence from
Jewish modes of interpreting Scripture, the Christians, Collins claimed,
had no other recourse than to return to the rabbis for their exegetical
deliverance. The scoundrel Collins could not have invented a better script
than this!

Far be it from me to view Collins in a different light. I will leave it to
the experts on Anthony Collins's work to determine whether he was a
deist or an atheist, whether he was simply ironic or an honest-to-goodness
liar, and whether or not he indeed delighted in leaving in chaos the very
foundations of Christian identity rooted in prophetic exegesis. I simply
would like to read Collins in a different way, in relation to his sources,
that is, to the narrative of Michel de la Roche upon which Collins based
his summary of Surenhusius's book, and in relation to Surenhusius himself. And I would also like to ask another set of questions: Whether or
not Collins took Surenhusius seriously, did La Roche take him seriously,
and were there others in Collins's era who might not have regarded him
as the kook contemporary scholars seem to take him to be? I suspect, and
I wish to argue the point both in the remainder of this chapter and in the
next, that the project of Surenhusius had its followers both in England
and on the Continent. What might appear patently absurd to recent historians of Collins's thought might have seemed somewhat more credible
and worthy of consideration by at least some of Collins's readers. Collins
might indeed have been disingenuous in approvingly presenting Surenhusius's method, but this need not deny the fact that others approved it,
that it was deemed innovative by some in utilizing previously unexploited

hermeneutical tools for understanding foundational Christian texts, and that Surenhusius and his project were ultimately a significant part of a larger defining moment in the history of Christian thought and scholarship and in the history of Jewish-Christian interactions at the beginning of the eighteenth century.

Before turning to Collins's source in de la Roche and to the reception of Surenhusius's writing within the larger intellectual community, I will consider one more recent reading of the Whiston-Collins debate, a kind of theological-historical reflection that offers a somewhat different perspective than those I have considered so far, and along with it, two responses by Collins's contemporaries among the plethora of responses the debate evoked. The late Hans Frei offered his own reading of the debate in his *The Eclipse of Biblical Narrative*, which was published in 1974. Frei understood the debate between the two thinkers as one over fact claims and over the question of the appropriate hermeneutic for the Christian scholar. Collins, in his analysis, left only two alternatives. The rules of literal interpretation of Whiston deem the New Testament false. But nonliteral interpretation deems it meaningless because such an interpretation has nothing to do with the actual words of the prophecies. In Frei's formulation, Collins has left us with the option of literal and false or typological and meaningless.[16]

Frei enlists a contemporary of Collins, Thomas Sherlock (1677–1761), to argue that these two dichotomies do not exhaust the possibilities of faith for a believing Christian: "Those who consider the Prophecies under the Old Testament, as so many Predictions only, independent of each other, can never form a right Judgment of the Argument, for the Truth of Christianity . . . representing spiritual Blessings under the Images of temporal Prosperity, and oftentimes such Images as cannot possibly admit of a literal Interpretation. In which Case thou' we may see the general Intent and Meaning, and find sufficient Ground for Hope and Fear from the Scope of the Prophecy, yet we can have no Certainty to fix the precise and determinate Manner in which the Words are to be fulfilled." In other words, Sherlock argued that prophecies "are chiefly for our sake who live by Faith and not by Sight." Moreover, prophecy is not essential as evidence of the truth of divine revelation. God is under no requirement to reveal all of the secrets of his providence at all times, and therefore it is absurd to complain about the obscurity of ancient prophecies.[17]

Frei adds that Collins never came to grips with Sherlock's thought since, as a student of Locke, he identified the literal sense of prophecy with an actual historical reference. Historical statements were simply and solely empirical. There were only two kinds of ideas: those of sensation representing external substances and their qualities, and those of reflection, by which we apprehend our own minds. Any proposition has but one meaning, and interpretation of Scripture must conform to the rules of the meaningful use of language, so that a proposition cannot mean several things at the same time. For Frei, Collins's work and the issues it raised were significant in that they proclaimed the triumph of the historical-critical interpretation of the Bible. Whiston had insisted on doing Bible study in the same manner as that of the fellows of the Royal Society, where the new science, grounded in Lockean assumptions, would set the rules of biblical analysis as well. And Collins, of the same mindset in this regard, accepted Whiston's assumption while proposing, of course, although not seriously in Frei's estimation, the alternative of Surenhusius's reading. In seeing the text as only a source of fact claims and not meaning, both participants in the debate could not appreciate, as Sherlock had put it, that prophecies were intended for those "who live by Faith and not by Sight."

Frei might have considered another respondent to Collins who approached the issues of the debate from a different perspective than that of Sherlock, but who might have easily found common ground with the latter. He deserves mention in this context both because he appears on the list of Moses Marcus's associates, as I have previously discussed, and because he provides an important example of a significant churchman who took the methods of Surenhusius quite seriously. I refer to Edward Chandler (1668?–1750), the aforementioned bishop of Coventry and Lichfield, who like Sherlock, published a response to Collins soon after the appearance of his book. Unlike the others we have encountered up to now, with the exceptions of Surenhusius and Carpzov, Chandler was a serious scholar of Hebrew and Judaism. Every page of his volume is studded with references to relatively obscure Jewish sources, such as works by Joseph Albo, Moses Maimonides, David De Pomis, Elijah Levitas, Levi ben Gershon, and many more. He also cites Surenhusius several times, but most importantly, he seems quite comfortable with his approach. He openly approved the typological and allegorical readings of biblical prophecy dismissed by Whiston, and acknowledged, without any hesitation, that they were similarly understood by Jews: "That the antient and modern Jews understand many Texts of the Messias, as the Christians do, which are plainly typical." Since Matthew composed his gospel for Jews, Chandler added, "he might the more freely give into a method of citing the Jews [as they] had been accustomed to, and allude to Passages in their Scriptures, which were not to be taken for express Proofs." It follows, in Chandler's estimation, that the allegorical method employed by the Jews is legitimate for Christians as well, since it was sometimes used by the writers of the New Testament themselves. And thus on Paul, he adds, "To the Jew he became a Jew even in the Method of Discoursing and Writing, to confirm them in the Truth." Surenhusius, as we shall see, could not have stated it better.[18]

If Collins had expected his readers to take his presentation of Surenhusius as a joke on Christianity, Chandler, for one, did not see it that way, nor did Michel de la Roche, who provided Collins with a well-crafted summation of Surenhusius's arguments, presented with the utmost respect and admiration. It is time we now consider de la Roche, his work, and his narrative of Surenhusius, and beyond his narrative, Surenhusius himself.

Michel de la Roche (c. 1680–1742) was a French Huguenot who settled in England via Holland. In 1701, he was received into the Anglican Church and was naturalized as an English citizen soon after. In subsequent years, he traveled widely in Europe, sustained a long relationship with Pierre Bayle, and even translated a part of his *Dictionaire* into English. His primary contribution to cultural life was his literary journals, produced in both French and English, which served as major conduits of scholarly information through highly informative reviews of books on the Continent for English readers and visa versa, for French readers. In all of these journals, the *Bibliotheque Angloise,* the *Memoires litteraires de la Grande Bretagne, Memoirs of Literature, New Memoirs of Literature,* and *A Literary Journal,* de la Roche consistently advocated toleration and freedom of thought, attacking religious persecution wherever he found it. He was particularly eager to publicize the well-known cases of Catholic and Calvinist intolerance such as those of Michael Servetus and Sebastian Castello, as well as the less known Nicolas Anthoine, as we shall see shortly. Through his European travels he established contact with a wide range of intellectuals with similar political and religious proclivities, such as Jean-Alphones Turrettin and Jean Robert Chouet in Geneva, Antonio Magliabecchi in Italy, Jacques Cappellus, the son of Louis Cappellus in France, and the leading members of the Huguenot community in London. He was clearly connected ideologically with the Latitudinarians in England, especially Samuel Clarke, William Whiston, and Benjamin Hoadley, and was in sympathy with their unorthodox views.[19]

Even a quick perusal of some of the many reviews in his journals provides the distinct impression of his remarkable interest in biblical and Hebrew studies, as well as religious history and theology. He reviewed, for example, the history of the Jews of Jacques Basnage; a work on ancient Hebrew poetry published in Padua; a tract of Maimonides concerning the red heifer by Andrea Zellero; a new Hebrew grammar without points by M. Masclef; William Lowth's commentary on Isaiah; the collected works of John Selden, edited by David Wilkins; a Latin translation of the tractate Sukkah of the Mishnah, and much more.[20]

He was well aware of the Whiston-Collins debate, and although he was a friend of Whiston, he treated the broad issues both men raised with fairness, notwithstanding his own role in the controversy regarding Suren-husius. In his *New Memoirs of Literature,* de la Roche reviewed Whiston's *Supplement to the Literal Accomplishment of Scripture,* published in 1725, faithfully reporting Whiston's position that no prophecy can have a double sense and his condemnation of Jerome, "a principal introducer of Anti-Christianism into the Church," for having been "the great instru-ment" of these double-sense interpretations.[21] In the next issue, he re-viewed at great length one of the many responses to Collins's *Discourse* written by Arthur Ashley Sykes (c. 1684–1756), the rector of Rayleigh in Essex. De la Roche reported that Sykes acknowledged Whiston's point about the impossibility of applying a prophecy to two different persons. The Isaiah prophecy, for example, is "very agreeable to the miraculous birth of Jesus, and not as a prophecy of his birth."[22]

He also summarized two other critical points of Sykes's analysis. The first underscored the importance of studying rabbinic literature in read-ing the New Testament, a position de la Roche strongly supported with-out mentioning Surenhusius directly: "But we must enter into the Jewish Phraseology, and see what the Jews meant by such and such expressions, and upon what principles they reasoned. Their ways of speaking and of quoting, which can be learned from Jewish writers only, must be look'd into; and how unnatural so ever they may seem to us, we must be deter-mined by them." Sykes's second point was to argue that fulfillment of a prophecy need not necessary imply its full completion, but only "as a re-semblance of facts." Thus differences of words and phrases in the accounts of the prophecies will be more easily accepted. In any case, no one should argue "from such allusions, applications, or resemblances, as if they were the grounds and reasons of the Christian religion." De la Roche was obvi-ously pleased by this book and praised its great service to Christianity. He also justified the length of the review since "it is certainly very proper that my Readers should find in this Journal something concerning the pre-sent Dispute about the Citations in the New Testament, a Dispute, which has made so great a Noise, not only among the Clergy, but also among the Laity; a Dispute which has employed the Pens of Bishops, Deans, Doctors of Divinity, and other learned Divines."[23]

Prior to publishing his long review of Surenhusius's study of rabbinic hermeneutics, which caught Anthony Collins's eye, de la Roche reviewed the six-volume edition of the Mishnah Surenhusius had published several years earlier, which included the original text and a Latin translation of the text, as well as the commentaries of Bertinora and Maimonides and the learned comments of Surenhusius himself. De la Roche describes the entire six tomes, giving full credit to the early translators of various trac-tates upon which Surenhusius had relied in finishing his edition. De la Roche does not completely hide his biases with respect to the rabbinic tradition. Nevertheless, he fully appreciated the value of this work, especially in understanding Christian Scripture: "Twas the genius of the Nation to be scrupulously exact, nay frequently superstitious in the Performance of their Duties. . . . However, there are Infinite Number of Passages, and sometimes entire Treatises, full of reasoning and good Sense." True wit, eloquence, and the sublime might be too much to expect from this work, he adds, but such a work as "the Perk Avoth" reveals considerable skill and judgment. He concludes: "The principal Advantage of this Work is to relate and explain the Opinions, Manners, Customs, Laws, Ceremonies, and Superstitions of the Jewish Nation in order chiefly to give us a right Understanding of the Scriptures, both of the Old and New Testament."[24]

It was some nine years before de la Roche got around to reviewing Surenhusius's ground-breaking study of rabbinic exegesis. When he did, however, he devoted considerable space to it and published it in three installments, one of which, as we shall see, was a digression, albeit a relevant one for de la Roche. He initially describes Surenhusius's work as "a Treatise, wherein the Passages of the Old Testament, quoted in the New, are vindicated and reconciled, according to the Forms of Quoting, and the several Ways of interpreting the Scripture used by the Ancient Hebrew Theologers." From the very beginning, de la Roche seems generally excited by this book. "Who would have thought," he writes, "that Rabbinical and Talmudical Learning would have occasioned such an excellent Performance? Mr. Surenhusius may be said to have raised a Noble and Magnificent Building out of Materials which appeared very contemptible and insignificant."[25]

De la Roche proceeds to offer a detailed summary of the preface to the work, explaining how Surenhusius was perplexed by the differences between the citations of the Old Testament and the New Testament, how he had spent considerable time with learned Jews discussing the problem, and how some had even volunteered to convert to Christianity if he could find a way of reconciling these seemingly corrupt citations. He finally met a rabbi learned in the Talmud and the Kabbalah, who had tried to convert to Christianity but had returned to Judaism; most importantly, the rabbi did not believe the New Testament was a corrupted book. Surenhusius then asked the rabbi to help him solve the impasse of citation that challenged so seriously the credibility of the New Testament. The rabbi proposed the following: "to peruse a great part of the Talmud, and the Allegorical and Literal Commentaries of the most Ancient Jewish Writers; to observe their several ways of quoting and interpreting the Scripture, and to collect as many Materials of that kind as would be sufficient for that Purpose."[26]

Surenhusius was inspired by the rabbi's ambitious project, and he launched a broad investigation presented in four sections to his readers.

He focuses on the different ways in which the rabbis cite biblical passages, how they refer to God, why passages are alleged to have been cited without being cited previously, and why some traditions are simply forgotten. Surenhusius soon realized how the Jewish exegetes took certain liberties in referring to the Old Testament, how "the authors of Gemara and ancient Allegorical writers change the literal sense into a noble and spiritual sense," and how they idiosyncratically presented their genealogies. What became evident to him the more he mastered his subject was that the writers of the New Testament "have done nothing in the present Case but what was practiced by the ancient Hebrew Theologers."[27]

If one might object to the use of later rabbinic literature to elucidate the New Testament's narrative form, Surenhusius would answer that the Jewish rabbinic tradition had remained relatively intact since its inception; the later materials had indeed preserved its ancient forms. Furthermore, there existed such conformity between the matter of quotations in the New Testament and in rabbinic literature that it was simply impossible that it could have happened by chance. De la Roche, despite his reluctance to appreciate rabbinic literature in its own right, has nothing but praise for this endeavor: "The Readers will admire the great Labour and Industry of the Author, and wonder that a Writer so full of Talmudical and Rabbinical Learning should have such a clear Head, and express himself with so much Perspicuity. I add, that they will thank him for those very things which they do not approve."[28]

In the second installment of his review of Surenhusius, de la Roche takes an unusual turn by introducing a subject close to his heart but hardly relevant, so it seems, to the Amsterdam scholar's work. Here is his justification for the digression:

As I was going to give a further Account of Mr. Surenhusius's Book . . . , it came to my Mind, that Nicolas Anthoine forsook the Christian Religion, and embraced Judaism, for no other Reason, but because he could not reconcile those two Genealogies, and the Quotations of the Evangelists and Apostles. A Book, like that of Mr. Surenhusius, would doubtless have prevented his Apostasy. I shall insert here the History of that Man that everybody may be the more sensible of the Usefulness and Importance of Mr. Surenhusius's Work; and I am apt to believe the second Extract of his Book will be more acceptable to the Readers, after they have read the following Piece.[29]

This was not the first time de la Roche had publicized the fascinating story of the Catholic Nicolas Anthoine, who had attempted to convert to Protestantism, then consulted Jews in Metz, Venice, and Padua before secretly converting to Judaism on his own, and was finally executed by the Church authorities of Geneva in 1632. In fact, de la Roche had published the story no less than four times, three times in English and once in French. He had so been fascinated by the story that he collected several contemporary accounts of it, including material from the archives in Geneva, presented them both in French and in English translation, and clearly advocated more humane treatment for those deviating from orthodox Christianity.[30]

Moreover, in an earlier description of Anthoine and his trial, de la Roche had previously linked Anthoine's apostasy to the contemporary debate on biblical prophecies involving William Whiston and one of his critics, Nicholas Clagett (1654–1727), the archdeacon of Sudbury and the rector of Hitcham, Suffolk. De la Roche explains "that he publishes this Piece in a time when Dr. Clagett thinks it necessary to put out a Vindication of those Christian Commentators, who have expounded some prophecies of the Messias not to be meant only of him. He makes this Observation, because the Ignorance of the double Sense of some Prophecies relating to the Messias was the chief Cause of Anthoine's Apostasy." In this instance, de la Roche most interestingly appears to promote the position contrary to that of his friend Whiston by declaring that some prophecies imply a double sense, and that had Anthoine appreciated that fact he may not have relinquished his Christian faith.[31]

In the present instance, de la Roche again linked the Anthoine story to the challenge of understanding the relationship between Old Testament prophecy and its fulfillment in the New. Anthoine's immoral treatment at the hands of the Calvinist authorities was the reason de la Roche was initially moved to write about his case. Yet having reported how the young man struggled to find meaning in his Christian identity and adopted Judaism instead, even after being spurned by contemporary Jews, de la Roche apparently had difficulty in understanding why the Christian faith had failed the man in the first place. Having focused on the Whiston debate and the problem of Christian prophecy, the books of Clagett and Surenhusius seem to have addressed not only an intellectual challenge but an existential one as well. If indeed Surenhusius was capable of making the New Testament credible by contextualizing it within rabbinic modes of interpretation and quotation, he had done a marvelous service to his fellow Christians, far more significant than solving a scholarly problem.

De la Roche fully understood that Christianity rose or fell on the matter of how the promises of biblical prophecy were fulfilled though its teaching. Christians had failed doubly in treating this bewildered man in his search for divine truth by murdering him and by previously not offering him the proper theological and exegetical guidance to return him to the right path. Defining Anthoine's failure to find meaning in the Christian faith as a matter of flawed exegesis and offering first the solution of Clagett and then that of Surenhusius made perfect sense for an editor consistently fascinated by the study of Hebrew and the Bible and committed to publicizing these matters in the pages of his journals.[32]

De la Roche then presented the full story of Anthoine based on the rich sources at his disposal. When the young man defiantly declares his allegiance to Judaism, it is framed in the context of the Christian failure to interpret the Old Testament properly: "I believe I am in the way to Truth and Salvation, and shall persevere in it, till I am shewed the contrary by good Reasons taken from the Old Testament." And de la Roche later repeats the point: "that he rejected the New Testament, because he found many Contradictions in it, and because it did not agree with the Old." De la Roche concludes this narrative by underscoring the same message: "It appears . . . that Nicolas Anthoine was a weak and extravagant Man for embracing Judaism because he could not fully reconcile the two genealogies of Jesus Christ, and several Passages of the Old Testament alleged in the New."[33]

De la Roche returns to Surenhusius's work in yet a third installment by immediately referring to the preface he had previously described as "so instructive, and so well adapted to the Design of his Work." He then summarizes the five parts of his work, demonstrating how Surenhusius had treated so comprehensively both of the matters on Antoine's mind: that of quoting Scripture and that of reconciling the various genealogies of Christ. He then turns to several specific examples taken from Surenhusius's text to illustrate the methods of citation in the New Testament against their rabbinic background. First he takes up the verses in Matt. 2:3–6 that purport to cite Mic. 5:2. He carefully demonstrates how Matthew reworked the Micah text with full awareness of the rabbinic rules of citation. In so doing, he "elegantly expresses the Sense of the Hebrew Text," for "the ancient Hebrew Doctors do not use to quote the very Words, but only to express the Sense." In a similar manner, the remainder of de la Roche's review is taken up with further examples illustrating a method of reading the New Testament passages in the light of parallel rabbinic texts that provide a common frame of reference for explaining peculiar stylistic extravagances and reading practices shared by both communities.[34]

Whatever Collins was to make of this method, there is no doubt that he had read a full report of it from a highly faithful and sympathetic reporter. If there was indeed deception on his part in presenting Surenhusius's book as a serious solution to the crisis of Christian exegesis, it did not come from de la Roche, who overcame his aversion to rabbinic literature to treat Surenhusius respectably and even enthusiastically. Rather than view his insertion of Nicolas Anthoine's life story as an unnecessary distraction that diminished the positive reception he had afforded Surenhusius in the first place, I would prefer to see it rather as an even stronger endorsement of what Christians required: new and bold scholarly tools to make sense of their own Scripture. Indeed the sad case of Anthoine underscored dramatically the urgency of such projects!

Collins would also have been hard pressed to imply that the scholar William Surenhusius (1666–1729), whom he had seemingly recruited for his cause was anything other than a highly learned and original authority, one increasingly noticed by his contemporaries both in England and on the Continent. He was in fact a scholar's scholar, hardly interested in participating in the polemical exchanges Collins and his contemporaries pursued almost as sport. He preferred instead the life of the mind, of editing texts and commenting about them in endless detail, in reading books, and in collecting a remarkable private library containing most of the major classical and contemporary Hebrew writings of Jewish authors.[35]

In many respects, the beautiful folio volumes of the Surenhusius Mishnah represent a culmination of over a hundred years of Christian scholarship on the classic Jewish code. Surenhusius built on the foundations of several earlier translators, whose work he graciously acknowledged. He faithfully translated the two most important Jewish commentaries of the text and then added his own elaborate one. His oration on the value of the study of the Mishnah rings with a deep appreciation of the rational methods of the rabbis, whose methods should be compared with those of Roman law. He also elicits a deep sense of Christian commitment, which is the driving force behind his decision to devote a lifetime of study to rabbinic texts. For Surenhusius, the Mishnah was the word of God. While Christians and Jews found different ways to express the divine will, they were ultimately connected in their faiths. A Christian Hebraist should not use his knowledge to vilify the Jewish tradition but should embrace the good fortune of having discovered this remarkable resource for the Christian faith. Surenhusius was proud of his close relations with Jews, and that they had been well treated in his native city. He was also in favor of Christian preaching among Jews so that Jews would come to know and appreciate Christianity more fully.[36]

In the final analysis, Surenhusius believed that rabbinic literature was more than a pragmatic scholarly resource through which Christianity's historical roots could be better understood. The Mishnah especially was part of the divine revelation, offering the key to reconciliation between Jews and Christians. Since ultimately the New Testament and the Mishnah ushered from the same divine source, Christians and Jews would join in the same faith through their mutual study. Surenhusius had not only brought Christian rabbinic learning to a new scholarly level; he had made textual study the ultimate spiritual task for Jewish-Christian rapprochement. Through the Mishnah Christians would be better able to recognize their true faith and Jews would come to understand as well that their rabbinic digest of laws ultimately conveyed a Christian truth. In Surenhusius's work, a new engagement in Jewish sources had provided Christians with a profound way of apprehending the testimony of their own faith through that of the Jews. By studying the Mishnah, a Christian might come to learn that the New Testament was indeed the fulfillment not the falsification of the Old. Centuries of acrimonious dispute could now be overcome through mutual study and respectful dialogue. In the end, the ultimate conversion of the Jews would be inaugurated through the efforts of the Christian scholars of Jewish texts.

Whether or not Collins fully appreciated the achievements of Surenhusius, whether or not he had been favorably convinced by the positive appraisal of de la Roche, he found the notion that rabbinic study could enrich Christian self-understanding to be at least worthy of mention, and he basically reported it to his readers as a reasonable alternative to Whiston's approach, without distorting or falsifying what de la Roche had provided him. It is true that he could not help himself from embellishing his narrative by comparing Surhenhusius's meeting with the rabbi to Luther's pact with the devil. And while Surenhusius's project has little to do with the "cabbalists," Collins had no hesitation in equating the figurative or typical way of reading Scripture to kabbalism, a kind of Judaic madness that Christian exegetes had willfully adopted. Collins may have stretched the truth somewhat to bring out a more cynical reading of his source, but his was still a relatively accurate and fair accounting of what de la Roche had said. It had been embraced by a man, theological liar though he may have been, who valued Jewish sources, read Jewish books, and even secured valuable Jewish manuscripts for his personal library.

One need not make the case that Collins was sincere in his use of Surenhusius to appreciate that this Dutch scholar had built a serious reputation among certain clerical circles throughout Europe. More importantly, when Collins wrote, the study of rabbinic texts was very much a passionate interest for a growing number of scholars, especially in England. They cited Surenhusius, they continued to apply and refine his methods, and they even initiated the difficult task of translating the Mishnah into the English language, as we shall see in the next chapter. By the first decades of the eighteenth century, the Christian study of rabbinics had been transformed from a relatively esoteric field of antiquarian scholarship to a more primary means of reinvigorating the study of Christianity itself. No serious Christian scholar could ignore this fact unless he was willing to face the peril of imperfectly understanding the foundations of his own faith.

Chapter 6

On the Proper Education of an English Divine: William Wotton and His Learned Friends

The primary exponent of the methods of Surenhusius on English soil was William Wotton (1666–1727). Wotton was a child prodigy, especially gifted in learning languages. It is said that he could read passages in Latin, Greek, and Hebrew at the age of five. He later acquired proficiency in Arabic, Syriac, and Aramaic, along with a broad education in several disciplines at Cambridge. In 1694, he gained considerable recognition in English and European learned society with the publication of his *Reflections upon Ancient and Modern Learning*, a thoughtful discussion of the merits of the moderns over the ancients in a variety of academic fields and literary endeavors, as well as a spirited defense of the Royal Society of which he was a fellow. Written as a response to William Temple's *Essay on Ancient and Modern Learning*, Wotton's book evoked numerous responses, pro and con, and was even satirized by Jonathan Swift in his *The Tale of a Tub* and in his *The Battle of the Books*. Yet Wotton's publication, which he later revised and defended, was highly regarded as one of the first comprehensive attempts to provide a history of the growth of scientific ideas. Wotton's role as a student of rabbinics is particularly interesting, as I shall argue, when considered in the light of his self-consciousness about living in a modern age, which he considered vastly superior to previous ones.[1]

Wotton's primary achievement in enhancing Jewish learning in England was the publication of his learned translation of two tractates of the Mishnah, including a long excursus on the value of rabbinic learning for Christians. While he labored on this project primarily on his own, he received the enthusiastic support of two of his close friends and colleagues, Simon Ockley (1679–1720) and the previously discussed David Wilkins, who was the chaplain of William Wake, the archbishop of Canterbury, and, of course, Moses Marcus's chief mentor and supporter in his conversion to Christianity. Ockley began his career in the study of Hebrew but eventually became known as an Arabist and as a historian of Islam. In many ways, he was inspired by Humphrey Prideaux, who had similarly worked in the fields of Hebraic and Arabic studies. We shall soon see how Prideaux clearly approved and blessed the intellectual achievements of both Ockley and Wotton in continuing his own life work. Ockley translated Leon Modena's *Riti* into English in 1707 under the title *A History of the Present Jews throughout the World*. He also translated the Arabic classic *The Life of Hayy ibn Yaqzan* by Ibn Tufayl, the fictional account of a solitary child growing up on an island in "a state of nature" and attaining a true natural religion. Refraining from writing directly on Muhammad, in deference to Prideaux and his famous history of the prophet, Ockley composed instead his pioneering two-volume history of the Saracens. In 1711, he was appointed to the chair of Arabic studies at Cambridge. He died at the age of forty-two in a state of declining health and fortune.[2]

On the basis of a large collection of letters written by Wotton and others to Ockley, now held both at the British Library and at Cambridge, it is possible to reconstruct the circumstances leading to Wotton's rabbinic publications and the involvement of his friends Ockley and Wilkins in this project. The earliest letter of relevance to this subject is one penned by Humphrey Prideaux to Simon Ockley on September 2, 1700. Prideaux was fully supportive of his young protégé Ockley and mentions that he had written on Ockley's behalf in support of his candidacy for the Hebrew lectureship at Cambridge. The letter offers some pedagogical advice on how Ockley might pursue the dual trajectories of his rabbinic and Arabic studies. The first part discusses the study of the Mishnah and is particularly significant in the light of Wotton's later project, undertaken without Ockley's direct involvement but with his strong support.

Here are Prideaux's instructions to Ockley:

If you read the *Mishnah* you cannot understand it without Commentary . . . Rabbi Yom Tob [Lipman Heller, 1579–1654] is the first critical Commentator and Rabbi Obadiah Bertinora [c. 1450–c. 1516] and Rabbi Moses Maimonides [1135–1204] both explain the sense intending of the books. Maimonides and Bertinora are printed together with the Text in a folio and Bertinora and Yom Tob with the font on three Quartos. Mr. Guise began to publish the *Mishnah* in Latin but died before he completed the first Book. That what was published may be had, and if you would finish what he hath begun, it would be a Work that the World needs but it will require time. Pray when you begin to read that book, do it with this view. Abendana made a sort of Translation of it at Cambridge where the Manuscript of it is in the University Library, and I think they got him there for it. . . . Maimonides' Commentary on the *Mishnah* was writ originally in Arabic [and] is more intelligible in that Language than in the Translation which is the Source of his Mistakes. But to make you thoroughly understand the *Mishnah* you should be well versed in Maimonides' *Yad* which is a most excellent Digest of Jewish Law as contained in the *Mishnah* and *Talmud*. To understand the Author, L'Emperour *Clavis Talmudica* will be useful. . . .[3]

Although Surenhusius's edition of the Mishnah had recently been published in Amsterdam, Prideaux had not yet heard of it. Nevertheless, the intellectual connections between him and the professor from Amsterdam are obvious. Prideaux both reveals his personal experience in reading the Mishnah with its traditional commentaries, along with Maimonides' code of Jewish law, and makes reference to a tradition of early scholarship that included Abendana, Guise, and L'Empereur. He proposes to Ockley that he devote himself to the project of translating the Mishnah, "a Work that the World needs," while, at the same time, pursuing his Arabic studies.

Although we have no indication of how Ockley responded to the letter of his esteemed mentor, it is apparent that he eventually chose a path that favored Arabic studies over Hebrew and never pursued the translation of the rest of the Mishnah. Yet the subject of the Jews, their rites, and their beliefs was still close to his heart. Only seven years later, he published his own translation of the famous apologia for Jewish life, written originally in Italian by the Venetian rabbi Leon Modena. Ockley based his translation on the French edition of Richard Simon, which also included two appendices on the Samaritans and Karaites. In his preface, Ockley provided a preview of the position he would strongly articulate in support of Wotton's rabbinic scholarship: "The Knowledge of the Jewish Rites and Customs is absolutely requisite for a true Understanding of the Old Testament; and of singular Use, and doth very much conduce, to a true and right Knowledge of the Christian Oeconomy. This is evident because so many Learned and Pious Divines, have employed a considerable Part of their Time and Study that way. It is also no less Entertaining than Advantageous, to observe the great Disparity between that Learned and Warlike People (once God's Peculiar Chosen) and who they now are."[4] Ockley's last thought might suggest that contemporary Jews presented by the rabbi represent an improvement over their "learned" but "warlike" ancestors, although "warlike" might not have been meant in a negative sense at all. Whatever the case, Ockley fully appreciates Jewish learning, including the study of contemporary Jewish life, as an absolute requisite for understanding the Bible and Christianity.

Six years passed before Wotton began to correspond regularly with Ockley about his intellectual projects. In a letter dated October 3, 1713, Wotton reports on his developing theory about the origin of languages in Babel. He reflects on the differences between Hebrew, Greek, and Arabic grammar and asks Ockley about the specific conjugations of certain Arabic roots. In the course of his description of what would eventually become a book, he mentions that the Mishnah is "one of the oldest uncannonical Books in any language to this day," and he claims that despite the introduction of new words and phrases by the rabbis, it is essentially written in the same language as that of Moses.[5]

He wrote again on March 7, 1714, apologizing for his long silence owing to illness. In the letter he alludes to Ockley's responses to his queries about his book on language and acknowledges how much Ockley has taught him. He then makes mention for the first time of another project he is planning: ". . . to print some other theological Essays of a miscellaneous Nature. Among others, in compliance to an Inquiry of a Gentleman who had some doubts concerning the Jewish Sabbath . . . I propose to print large Extracts of the Talmudic Massichtoth, Shabbath and Eruvim." Offering his opinion that the Mishnah and the traditions that it preserves are coeval with the New Testament, he turns to Ockley with the following request: "If you think it worth your while, I will be glad to have your Thoughts on the Torah Shebbeal Peh [the oral law] (As they call it at large). Two or three Sheets of Paper (It would not hurt you) would be a noble Addition to my Work. And I would have made to the Public as agreeable a Project as I can." He closes with a request for the opinions of the Jewish commentators Abravanel, Gersonides, and Naḥmanides on the confusion of tongues at Babel.[6]

Fourteen months later, on May 14, 1715, Wotton wrote again, expressing his joy over the fact that Ockley had agreed to write a letter "vindicating the History of the Mishnic [*sic*] tradition."[7] But despite Ockley's good intention to write, he had still not produced the letter by December 7, 1715, as we learn from Wotton's communication to Dr. Walker, a fellow of St. John's College in Cambridge.[8] Despite Wotton's pestering his colleague, he still did not have the letter when he again wrote to Dr. Walker on May 31, 1716, although Ockley had apparently apologized for the long delay. Wotton still provides an update on the progress of his two books: "A great Part of what I am doing is ready. I have some thoughts of having it printed in Cambridge, but I can't resolve upon that, though I long earnestly to do it, unless you can procure me somebody that will give himself the Trouble to correct the Press. I think to print two entire Titles of the Misna . . . in Hebrew and English, with a Commentary." He hints that he would have liked but did not expect Ockley to be his editor. He apologizes for making so many requests of his friends, but he is confident that the final product will be worthy of his endeavors and will leave its mark on Christian scholarship.[9]

With the passage of two more years, Wotton finally wrote on March 24, 1717 to thank Ockley for his "kind and friendly letter which you are pleased to express yourself so much to my advantage as to what I have said concerning the Authority of the Jewish Tradition."[10] He then reports in two letters written in May 1717 of the completion of his work, to be published in London in two volumes: "The First will contain the Discussion of Nature, Authority and Usefulness of the Mishna," while the second will contain his translation of Shabbat and Eruvim with his annotations.[11] A year later in 1718, he reflects on the project that is now behind him, admitting that the subject of Eruvim is indeed quite dry, but crediting himself, nonetheless, for having corrected the image of the Jews as stupid and inconsistent "among us *Notsorim* [Christians]," and thus deserving of their gratitude.[12]

Wotton's *Miscellaneous Discourses Relating to the Traditions and Uses of the Scribes and Pharisees in the Blessed Saviour Jesus Christ's Time* was eventually published in London in 1718. It was dedicated to William Wake, the archbishop of Canterbury, perhaps through the intervention of his house chaplain, David Wilkins, who was a strong supporter of the project. In the preface, Wotton explains the genesis of the work in a conversation he had with "a very ingenious Gentleman" about the origins of the observance of the Sabbath, and specifically among Christians. Dissatisfied with the existing literature on the subject, "I determin'd therefore to examine into the Traditions of the Elders, and to see how the Scribes and Pharisees in our blessed Saviour's Time commanded the Sabbath to be observed." When he examined their ancient texts, he was pleasantly surprised to find the Mishnah to be a most substantial work, notwithstanding the degree of contempt it has received from many learned men.[13]

Citing freely his predecessors in the Christian study of the Mishnah— William Guise, William Surenhusius, and John Lightfoot (1602–75)— he extols the work's integrity and reliability, so that "wherever it gives light to any Custom, Passage, or Phrase mentioned in the Old and New Testaments, its light may certainly be depended on." He also presents the dissonant view of Isaac Vossius (1618–89), who despised anything rabbinical and found the Greek Bible more reliable than the Hebrew, and Philo and Josephus more trustworthy than the rabbis. The rabbinical traditions are so corrupted, Vossius maintained, that the Jews can only ascertain their origins through Christian sources. Wotton brings in the refutation of Vossius' position by Richard Simon and acknowledges the earlier Latin translations of parts of the Mishnah by Johannes Cocceius, Constantijn L'Empereur, and Robert Sheringham.[14]

Wotton not only insists on the Mishnah's reliability; he sees it as a major source of understanding the phraseology and the larger background of the New Testament. He is thoroughly convinced, contra Vossius, that Josephus cannot provide a more reliable witness than the rabbis and adds an important confirmation of his opinion by the learned David Wilkins:

I am the more confirmed in my Opinion upon consulting my most learned Friend Dr. Wilkins (to whom the Publick are so much oblig'd for his late Edition of the Coptic Gospels) upon this very question, to which with great Humanity he gave me the most judicious Answer: "But the Talmudists, tho' they sometimes explain the Mosaic Law contrary to the Intention of the inspired Writers. By mollifying Punishments and precepts, and by magnifying Rewards and promises, yet they never misrepresent the Original, either by supplying other Words, or by adulterating the Text, which they keep religiously Sacred. But wherever both of them [the rabbis and Josephus] contradict the express Letter of the Law, I would still have more regard for the Misnic Writer than for Josephus, because the different Explication of the former tends perhaps towards establishing another probable Reason found in some other Place in the Scripture, and not express'd in the Text, of which he then treats . . . but in Josephus, you often find him introduce Novelties unheard of. . . ." So far this excellent Person, in whose Determination I entirely acquiesce.[15]

The citation of Wilkins by Wotton is important for several reasons. It confirms their close friendship and the warm respect Wotton paid his learned colleague. It also corroborates what we already know about Wilkins' command of rabbinic texts, acknowledged by another serious scholar of rabbinic literature in his own right. It patently attests to Wilkins' approval of Wotton's project, in his belief that the study of the Mishnah does enhance an understanding of the New Testament and early Christian origins. I might also suggest that Moses Marcus, Wilkins' own protégé, could have been aware of Wotton and his project through Wilkins' involvement, although, as I have indicated already, he probably had reservations about it.

One additional observation about Wilkins' carefully crafted remark is in order. His endorsement of the use of the Mishnah over the works of Josephus is not offered unreservedly and wholeheartedly. Note his declaration that the Talmudists "sometimes" explain the Mosaic Law in a manner "contrary to the Intention of the inspired Writers." Nevertheless, they "never misrepresent the Original, either by supplying other Words, or by adulterating the Text," and because they transmit the biblical text so faithfully, they are less prone to introduce novelties than Josephus. Wilkins' endorsement of the Mishnah with reservations might recall Moses Marcus's own position regarding the rabbis and rabbinic literature, especially as he articulates it in his introduction to Carpzov's work. He defends them there as sacred guardians of the authentic biblical text while casting aspersions on their notion of the oral law. Wilkins, it would seem from this passage, also focuses essentially on the rabbis as faithful transmitters of the Hebrew Bible, thus endorsing the Mishnah project in a more narrow and constricted way than either Wotton or Ockley. In this respect, his perspective on the rabbis is closer to that of Marcus; it is filled with ambivalence and reservations about openly acknowledging the value of rabbinic literature in general for Christian scholars.

Having provided, nevertheless, a positive endorsement of the Mishnah's authenticity from so distinguished a source, Wotton is still obliged to admit that "an impudent blending of the Misnic Text with the impertinent and fabulous, and ridiculous Glosses of the Doctors of both the Schools, but chiefly of the Babylonia, has . . . hurt the Authority of the

Misnic Text." But, nevertheless, a significant Christian scholarly community devoted to its study had "vindicated it from scorn and neglect" in the author's time. This community includes such scholars as Joseph Scaliger, John Selden, Robert Sheringham, Edward Pococke, John Lightfoot, and William Guise.[16] Wotton had carefully situated himself in a living tradition of Christian scholarship, albeit with a clear distinction between the utility of the study of the Mishnah and that of the Talmud. This distinction clearly served the interests of Christianity in focusing on a work closer to the era of the New Testament. In the study of the Mishnah Christian Hebraists also found a simpler, more accessible, and more straightforward text than kabbalistic and talmudic ones. Nevertheless, one wonders how valid such a contrast is between a legitimate rabbinic legal text and an illegitimate one. No doubt the Christian turn to the Mishnah as a source of Christian insight was a minor revolution in itself given the long centuries of scorn and indifference especially to rabbinic law, as distinguished from rabbinic homiletics, exegesis, and esotericism. But this revolution still had its limits. The rabbis of the Mishnah wrote good laws only to be soiled and corrupted by their talmudic successors! Nevertheless, despite Wotton's formulation, much of the scholarly community to which he referred and its successors—men like Surenhusius himself, John Selden, John Lightfoot, Edward Chandler, and David Wilkins too—simply ignored Wotton's sharp division between the ur-tradition of the rabbis and the later one. If one peruses their voluminous notes citing talmudic, medieval, and contemporary legal works, it is obvious that Wotton's limits to the Christian study of Jewish law could often be breached.

Whether each of these predecessors of the late sixteenth century and the seventeenth studied Mishnah alone or rabbinical literature in general, Wotton proudly regarded his own scholarship as a direct continuation of all of theirs. He not only refers to them throughout his text but uses both a special chapter (chapter 1) and a closing appendix to list each of their contributions.[17] The work of the early eighteenth-century scholars of the Mishnah, as Wotton and certainly Surenhusius saw it, was to continue what the pioneers of the previous century had begun. The case has already been effectively made by Lightfoot, Selden, and Pococke for the scholarly importance of rabbinic scholarship in illuminating ancient Christian literature and religion. It was up to Wotton and his colleagues to complete the task.

Yet if Wotton and his colleagues were mere disciples and successors of these seventeenth-century giants of Hebraic scholarship, was there indeed any significant difference between the achievements of the earlier generation and those of the later? Despite his sincere acknowledgment of indebtedness to those Christians who had paved the way in excavating rabbinic culture, in what way did Wotton actually consider his achievement distinct from theirs?

In many ways, Wotton and his contemporaries had hardly surpassed the most dramatic achievements of their predecessors, especially the English ones. Lightfoot's commentary on the New Testament, mining rabbinic sources to illuminate the Jewish background of early Christianity, was surely a model of what Wotton sought to achieve in his own work. Even more impressive were the stellar achievements of John Selden, appropriately called by Jason Rosenblatt "Renaissance England's Chief Rabbi." Wotton's masterful commentary on the Mishnah still paled in significance to Selden's half-dozen immense and highly learned tomes on rabbinic literature. Most important of all was Selden's contribution to international law, *De Jure Naturali et Gentium juxta Disciplinam Ebraorum,* published in 1640, a dramatic acknowledgment of the universal validity of the rabbinic Noachide laws as identical with the law of nature. In this daring work, Selden even placed rabbinic law over biblical law, deflating the biblical Ten Commandments as intended only for the Jews while elevating the Noachide laws, the novel construction of the rabbis, as binding upon all of humankind. Selden, as Rosenblatt makes abundantly clear, appreciated the rabbis and genuinely enjoyed their learning for its own sake with few theological axes to grind in a way that none of his contemporaries even approached.[18]

Selden's exceptional attitude toward rabbinic Judaism among Christian Hebraists might be usefully compared with that of Lightfoot, who more typically expressed his marked ambivalence to reading the rabbis in the preface to his commentary on the New Testament:

There are no authors that do more affright and vex the reader; and yet there are none who do more entice and delight him. In no writers is greater or equal trifling; and yet in none is greater or so great benefit. The doctrine of the Gospel hath no more bitter enemies than they; and yet the text of the Gospel hath no more plain interpreters. To say all in a word, to the Jews, their countrymen, they recommend nothing but toys, and destruction, and poison; but Christians, by their skill and industry, may render them most usefully serviceable to their studies, and most eminently tending to the interpretation of the New Testament.[19]

Wotton's position would appear closer to that of Lightfoot than that of Selden, particularly in his preference for the Mishnah over the Talmud and in his own awkward attempts not to identify too fully with his rabbinic subject. Yet despite the obvious similarity in approach, Wotton and his contemporaries, writing more than half a century after Selden and Lightfoot had produced their impressive scholarship, were not merely replicating what had been done by the early pioneers of their field. In fact, one might argue that they were self-consciously aware that their publications represented an advance over those of the previous generation. In the first place, they wrote with a greater self-assurance that their new work was significant because of its linkage to the efforts of the giants who preceded them. They were not creating a new field; they were continuing a scholarly tradition that had been fully legitimated and regularized within the scholarly community in which they participated. At the same time, they produced their work with a greater urgency than in previous generations because they thought, more than ever before, that Christianity could only be fully understood and legitimated through their scholarship. In the wake of the exegetical crisis engendered by historicism and philology that had been so dramatically displayed in the public debate between Whiston and Collins, they understood more acutely than ever before the immense value of rabbinic learning for Christian self-understanding. And most importantly, by beginning the process of translating the Mishnah into English, they also grasped the import of their work in reaching beyond the coterie of scholars who wrote in Latin to a wider readership of vernacular literature. Selden and Lightfoot had written to elite Latinists. In the new cultural world of the early eighteenth century, their findings along with those of their successors now accessible in English were to reach a wider lay readership through the efforts of Wotton and his circle of collaborators.

Following Wilkins's note, Wotton presented the letter from Simon Ockley, dated March 15, 1717, the letter he had expended considerable effort to solicit and to which he had thanked Ockley personally nine days later. The letter is important as an unambiguous and powerful endorsement of the study of rabbinics by Christians. Wotton was surely overjoyed by the directness with which Ockley composed his remarks and by the personal support he had finally received from his Cambridge friend:

We are obliged to you, for having evinced beyond all Contradictions that Hebrew Learning is necessary for us Christians. If I had ever had an Opportunity, I wou'd most certainly have gone thro' the New Testament under a Jew . . . that they understand it infinitely better than we do. They are thoroughly acquainted with all the Forms of Speech, and all the Allusions, which (because they occur but rarely) are obscure to us, tho' in common use and very familiar among them; as has been admirably demonstrated by the learned Surenhusius in his *Reconciliator.* I remember having read in F. Simon . . . in the Appendix to Leo Modena, that he once offered the Epistle to the Hebrews in Hebrew to a learned rabbi in Paris, who "after he had perused it, without taking any manner of notice of the difference in Religion, said, that whosoever was the Author of that Book, he was a great Mekubbal [a Jewish mystic] and thoroughly versed in all the Traditions of the Jewish Nation." . . . We do not make use of the Opinions of modern Rabbis, nor their uncertain Conjectures for the Confirmation of any Thing. But when we find Expressions and Allusions exactly the same with those in the New Testament; several Petitions in the Lord's Prayer; and some of our Lord's Parables in the Talmud: Are we to suppose that they came thither by Chance; or which is most ridiculous, that the Jews borrow'd them from the Christians; or rather which is the only true way of accounting for them, that they were in familiar Use among the Jews in our blessed Saviour's Time? . . . The Misna is undoubtedly a very venerable piece of Antiquity; collected with great Judgment, and digested with utmost exactness by that great and learned Rabbi, Judah, a Person, than whom none since the Destruction of the Temple, that we know of, had greater Advantages both of Wisdom, Learning, Riches, and Interest to furnish him with all the Materials necessary for the compleating so great a Work.[20]

This is the most conspicuous and earnest affirmation of the Surenhusius project we have yet seen from any contemporary, articulated in the most provocative of language, sure to be noticed by even the most indifferent of readers. Ockley refers to Surenhusius's book only four years after its publication, and seven years before Collins's endorsement would give it the notoriety its author had never sought. But it was not merely the mention of Surenhusius and his hermeneutical program that was tantalizing. It was Ockley's goading assertion that Jews could understand the New Testament "infinitely better than we do," and that if Ockley ever had the opportunity, he would most certainly have chosen a Jew to teach him the foundational text of his faith. Did Ockley actually understand the implications of the message he was broadcasting? Perhaps he had, when he reminded his reader that "we do not make use of the Opinions of modern Rabbis" for the confirmation of anything regarding the Christian faith. Nevertheless, wasn't he referring to actual living Jews when he recommended finding a suitable teacher to teach Christians their own holy book? And wasn't that the point of the Richard Simon story in which Simon enlisted a "great Mekubbal" to make perfect sense of the Epistle to the Hebrews?

If Anthony Collins had written these lines, it would surely have been offered as testimony of his theological lying by modern historians. But this was Simon Ockley, distinguished Cambridge professor, who purposely avoided high society because of his lack of ease in the company of politicians and socialites, who eschewed a close public relationship with William Whiston because of his alleged Arianism,[21] and who sometimes expressed concern about how he was perceived in the public eye, as we shall see shortly below. After Ockley had delayed the writing of his promised letter to Wotton for several years, even Wotton himself could not have expected such a bombshell. Ockley stated more bluntly than any Christian theologian before him how critically Christians needed Jews and their religious traditions in order to understand themselves. It is all the more remarkable that Ockley composed these lines given that he had made a conscious choice to devote himself to Islamic studies rather than Judaic. Perhaps he was expressing so firm a conviction as compensation for his scholarly choice or because he had less to lose, not being a scholar primarily in this field.

Having concluded his preface with Ockley's stimulating letter, Wotton opens the first volume of his publication which he calls *A Discourse Concerning the Nature, Authority, and Usefulness of the Misna or Body of the Traditional Laws of the Jews.* He begins with a systematic history of Christian scholarship on the Mishnah, culminating in his hero Surenhusius: "At last, Guilielmus Surenhusius, now Professor of Hebrew and Greek in what they call Schola Illustris in Amsterdam, undertook to give us the Misna entire in Hebrew and Latin. . . . The Greatness of the Undertaking deterr'd other Men, which makes our Obligation to him so much greater." He next offers a list of previous Christian students of Maimonides' law code, including "the excellent Dean of Norwich Dr. Prideaux, to whom this Generation are not a little oblig'd for his Connexion of the History of the Old and New Testament." While appreciating the value of previous work on Maimonides, he points out that the sections of the code that have been studied generally eschew an interest in ritual, thus failing to contribute significantly to an understanding of the "Traditions of the Elders."[22]

Wotton follows with a sweeping description of the Mishnah text and the nature of rabbinic logic, including a discussion of the *middot*, "the thirteen ways of reasoning, by which the masters draw their decisions from the Text of the Written Law." On the notion that these principles derived their sanctity from Sinai, he cannot restrain himself but to call this a whim. He is able to appreciate the modes of the rabbis' logical reasoning, but he is unable to acknowledge their divine status as representing the will of God. Nevertheless, he acknowledges that the rules "served them however for many useful (and I might add, sometimes for Knavish) Purposes, and helped to give a Sanction to many of their forced Interpretations of Scriptural Texts, by which they endeavour'd to support their Traditions." Aligning the Christians with the Sadducees and the Karaites who rejected the oral law, he launches a rigorous attack on the latter, offering several examples of convoluted, contradictory, and prevaricating interpretations of the rabbis, falsely attempting to ground their legal rulings in divine authority. His best example of rabbinic knavery he leaves for the end, the example of the Prosbul of Hillel:

This last Evasion lets us into the whole Mystery of the Traditional Law of the Elders. There appears in every part of it a wonderful Desire of being scrupulously exact in the most particular Niceties that related to the Law, and the Letter of it was most strictly kept to: And yet at the same time while they seem'd to adhere to the minutest Punctilio's of the written Text, they found ways to break it, when their Interest, or their Inclinations interfered. And where they determin'd to oppose the Law, right or wrong, a Constitution of Moses from Mount Sinai did the Business. This fully appears by our blessed Lord's description of their Hypocrisy and Injustice in the Gospels; and is exactly verified in the Misna itself, as we have already seen.[23]

The challenge to Wotton, as to every Christian advocate of rabbinic learning, was how to balance the positive features of its literature and mores with a total and complete rejection of its alleged divine status. This Wotton does by acknowledging the rationality of the rabbis' legal system while pointing out that "their Fault lay in claiming a greater Authority to them than they cou'd justly warrant."[24] In a similar manner, he will not overstate his case by claiming that the New Testament requires rabbinic understanding to unpack it. Christianity can never appear to be so subservient to Judaism. Rather, he makes more modest claims than Ockley and Surenhusius about the Mishnah: "It is highly useful and extremely pleasant" to contextualize New Testament utterances with rabbinic data, he argues; in fact, it is much more satisfactory that relying on Christian interpreters alone.[25] A Christian also has the added advantage of polemicizing with Judaism from within its own literature and can demonstrate the fraudulent claims of the oral law.

The balancing act that Wotton maintains between appreciating Jewish law without accepting its pretensions to speak with the same voice as the Bible distinguishes his position somewhat from that of Surenhusius. The Dutch professor sincerely maintained that both the New Testament and the Mishnah were divine; they were simply two faces of the same unitary truth. The Christian who masters the Mishnah actually comes to know the will of God, as does the Jew who reads the New Testament through the lens of his own tradition. This is not the case for Wotton. The Mishnah can never contain theological truth for the Christian. He can never accept its premises that it speaks with the same voice as the written law and represents what God actually willed. But he can accept its historical claims to truth. As a means of more deeply understanding the text and context of the New Testament, it is invaluable: "In short, the Authority of the Misna, to us Christians, is wholly historical; and being stampt with the Seal of the Jewish Nation . . . it certainly proves the Existence of any Usage in Question in its own time. . . . We have a faithful Representation of the Body of Traditions which were so severely censured, where they deserved it, by Jesus Christ when he was here on Earth."[26]

For Wotton, there are accordingly two kinds of truth claims: the divine and the human, or to put it another way, the theological and the historical. Secular history can now work to clarify faith, although it can never claim to know all the truth or the absolute truth that only God knows. Historical knowledge is valuable to the theologian as long as it functions within rules and limits. Historical truth can never be identical to theological truth, nor can the claims of the former ever overturn those of the latter.

Within the realm of historical truth, Wotton presents the Pharisees in a more nuanced way than their representation in the Gospels. He claims that Jesus did not find fault with their sect, only with the "Hypocricy, Knavery, and Cruelty" of many of its members. Jesus rebuked the Pharisees but never shunned them, and while Christians and Jews were alienated from each other for over a thousand years, the "Partition-Wall" has now been lifted in this generation, whereby Christians now have free access to the "useful and esteemable" part of the Jewish traditions.[27]

Wotton devotes the rest of the volume to a factual presentation of each of the mishnaic tractates, describing each of their contents in detail. These sections, quite similar to later introductions on rabbinic literature written by Jews for internal Jewish purposes, could have even been read and appreciated by Jewish students initiating their own religious education. He then offers a discourse on the daily recital of the Shema, explains the use of phylacteries and the mezuzah, and finally considers the original subject that prompted him to write the book: the meaning of the Jewish Sabbath and its Christian analogue, the Lord's day, which is Sunday. As an appendix to his book, he pays tribute to his predecessors with a list of all of the previous scholars who had translated the Mishnah into Latin.[28]

Before concluding the discussion of Wotton's *Miscellaneous Discourses,* one additional piece of evidence deserves to be mentioned. In light of the relatively esoteric nature of Wotton's work, including the actual text of the Mishnah itself, its readership was bound to be limited, and even Wotton had no illusions about how dry it was to actually study the Jewish law code. Yet was it possible that his book, especially its plea for the Christian study of rabbinic texts, might still have some impact on a larger community of English readers? I have been unable so far to track its influence in full, although I did discover one reference that suggests that the subject it featured might have interested more than a small coterie of linguistically talented specialists such as Wotton and Ockley.

In a letter sent to Simon Ockley by Rev. Nathaniel Spinckes on April 14, 1718, Spinckes apologizes to Ockley about the delay in sending him a certain sum of money he had requested from a Mr. Turner, but he then turns to another request Ockley had made of him, namely to inquire about a reference to his letter printed in the Wotton volume. Spinckes writes: "The Passage relating to Yourself that you inquire after is in Mr. Colliers 1st part of his Vindication of the Reasons and Defence, p. 45 in these words: 'The celebrated Orientalist Mr. Ockley, Arabick Professor at Cambridge, shall close the evidence. The Testimony is in his Letter to Dr. Wotton, and stands in the Postscript of the Volume last cited (Miscellaneous Discourses, etc.).'" What follows is a citation of a generous portion of Ockley's remarks, including his praise of R. Judah, the editor of the Mishnah. Spinckes then adds: "This is the whole of what is said of you; whereby you will clearly see there was no Disrespect assigned you but only that he was willing to shelter himself with your Authority of one so well versed in Jewish Affairs. . . ."[29]

The obscure reference Spinckes tracked down for Ockley is found in a work by Jeremy Collier (1650–1726), a bishop of the church of English non-jurors, a polemicist against the alleged immorality of the theater, and a champion of the independence of clerical authority over civil. Preferring the prayers regarding the Eucharist as prescribed in the first liturgy of Edward VI of 1549 over the present one in use of 1662, he tried to introduce a revised prayer book containing certain "Usages" deriving from the Roman one. Collier insisted that using this liturgy did not imply any assent to the doctrines of the Catholic Church and proceeded to impose it on his congregation in 1717. In his *Vindication of the Reasons and Defence,* Collier defended himself against his critics, especially the same Nathaniel Spinckes, the head of the "non-usagers," by displaying considerable erudition in support of his choices, including the use of rabbinic sources. In so doing, he offers the testimony of good Protestant divines who recommended the use of Jewish sources, including Brian Walton, Humphrey Prideaux, and John Lightfoot. In the last case, he cites Lightfoot's recommendation "that the best way of searching out the Sense of the many obscure Places in the New Testament, is to enquire in what Sense those Phrases and Manners of Speech were understood according to the common Dialect of that Nation: that this Enquiry could succeed no other way, than by consulting Talmudick Authors who both speak the vulgar Dialect, and reveal all Jewish Matters." Collier then mentions Wotton's very recent volume and the aforementioned citation of Ockley.[30]

That Ockley had bothered to inquire about the reaction to his letter on the part of a relatively unimportant clergyman is interesting in itself. It reveals, as I have indicated above, his very thin skin and his general avoidance of being in the limelight. He also probably was sensitive to the fact that he had taken a strong stand, articulated in a most provocative manner. Since the citation of his words only affirmed a positive reaction to what he had written and placed his in a long line of similar authoritative testimonies, he must have been relieved. Collier, of course, had little direct interest in writing on the rabbis, and the fact that he troubled himself at all to use and justify their literature had mostly to do with arguing his case on the value of including some prayers in the Anglican service. But his citation provides, nevertheless, an interesting example of how the use of rabbinic materials, though still controversial and still requiring the vindication of noted authorities, was entering the consciousness of a larger segment of the clerical community, surely beyond the bounds of the trained Hebraists such as Ockley and Wotton themselves.

Wotton himself desired that the agenda of rabbinic study by Christians become the common property of clerics far beyond his limited circle of friends and colleagues. In a more general work addressed to a wider readership entitled *Some Thoughts Concerning a Proper Method of Studying Divinity* (written only a few years before his *Miscellaneous Discourses* had appeared but published only posthumously in 1734), Wotton turned his attention to the matter of theological education. He was just as emphatic in this context as he had been in his special work on the Mishnah regarding the critical importance of Hebrew and rabbinics in the education of the Christian divine. Writing only a short time after Surenhusius's book on rabbinic hermeneutics had appeared, he eagerly recommends it to students preparing for the clergy. But first he mentions his edition of the Mishnah: "If he (our student) has a mind thoroughly to understand those Traditions of the Scribes and Pharisees, for which they are so severely rebuked by our blessed Saviour in the Evangelists, he will find a compleat System of them in Surenhusius's Edition of the Misna with the Commentaries of Maimonides and Bartenora. . . . It is a noble and authentick Collection of what the Jews have built upon Moses's Law in every particular."[31] Later, he prominently features Surenhusius' second work:

There he particularly shews how our blessed Saviour and his Disciples prov'd what they said out of Moses, and the Prophets, and why they quoted every Passage that they thought proper for their Purpose, in the particular Manner in which we see it alleged. He compares their Methods of Argumentation with those which are used by the Jewish Masters; and thereby demonstrates the Cogency of many Arguments produced by St. Paul which have perplexed most Christian Interpreters, and so shows the Connections between the Covenants in a fully and convincing Manner. And tho' his design led him to quote the Hebrew Text at every Turn, yet his Work is so contrived, that those that do not understand Hebrew, need not be frightened since most of his Allegations are exactly translated, and by that Means the Thread of his Arguments may be very easily comprehended.[32]

That Wotton had familiarized himself with Surenhusius' work so soon after its publication is impressive enough. That he recommends it so emphatically as part of a curriculum for students of theology, even if they cannot read Hebrew, offers eloquent testimony of its importance for Christian pedagogy. But reading Surenhuius's works is only a small part of the Jewish education Wotton seeks to impart to his potential students.

His list of recommended books and authors represents a virtual library of resources on the subject available in his day. They include Grotius, le Clerc, Pococke, Lightfoot, Dr. Allix, and even the polemics against Christianity of "Orobio the Jew."[33] The education of the Christian cleric in Judaism consists of mastery of ancient literature along with a familiarity with contemporary Jewish life: "If one would know the customs of that nation at this Day which are very well worth knowing: F. Simon's Translation of Leo Modena's Tract of the Rites and Ceremonies of the Jews [he strangely fails to mention his colleague Ockley's recent translation of the work], Fleury on the Manners of the Jews (which is an admirable little book), and Buxtorf's Synagoga Judaica."[34]

Yet reading the secondary accounts of the primary sources of ancient Judaism and Christianity are not sufficient for Wotton to demonstrate the profound interrelationship between the two faiths and their respective literary traditions. Wotton returns again to consider the Mishnah edition of Surenhusius, this time to provide hands-on advice on how to use this resource as one reads the New Testament. In reading these amazing instructions, we have moved from the realm of theory to practice, from the setting of theological discussion and debate to that of a teacher and his classroom. Here are Wotton's specific instructions to students:

I would advise him to read the respective Titles in the Misna in the order of which they lie in the Pentateuch without any regard to the Order in which they be in the Misna itself. As for instance, when the Chapter of the Waters of Jealousy, in the fifth of Numbers, or that of taking a Brother's Wife, in the 25th of Deuteronomy, are read in the Pentateuch; then the titles Sota and Jevammoth which correspond to those Laws, shou'd be read in the Misna, and so of the rest. The Misna and its Commentators will appear very dry, and perhaps ridiculous at first to men wholly unacquainted with that Learning, but Use will soon conquer that, and the Benefit which will thence arise towards the Understanding of the Mosaic Law, will abundantly compensate the Pains; and I speak from Experience, that all the Christian Commentators put together (at least those I have used) will not get a tenth Part of the Light to the Understanding the Law of Moses, that may be had by the Help of the Jewish Traditions.[35]

Wotton cautions, however, that this method should be tried only on advanced students of the Pentateuch so that "it will then be easier, pleasanter, and more profitable."[36] The rest of Wotton's instructions on clerical education are taken up with bibliography in other fields, such as books against the deists, Catholics, and other enemies of the Church. Nevertheless, the conspicuous place Wotton affords Judaic education, and specifically the study of the Mishnah, is striking. He clearly had not compartmentalized his interest in the subject to one well-researched book but considered it a vital dimension of Christian education in general, as this fascinating pamphlet readily illustrates.

Finally, before closing this chapter, I will consider briefly the book upon which most of Wotton's fame was established, his *Reflections Upon Ancient and Modern Learning*, which was first published as early as 1694. The book appeared some twenty-five years before his study of the Mishnah, so it does not reflect the knowledge and the scholarly resources Wotton had acquired in the course of so many more years of research, although it was updated in several subsequent editions. Nevertheless, it is clear that even in this early work, Wotton already valued Hebrew and rabbinic learning and regarded them as special accomplishments of his own generation. In the context of his advocacy of the significance of the learning of the moderns over the ancients, he writes the following:

It has been observed already, that scarce any of the Fathers understood Hebrew besides Origin and St. Hieron. . . . For which Reasons, Syriac, Chaldee, Samaritan, and Arabic, have been studied by modern Critics; not to mention the Writings of the Rabbins and the Talmudists, to which the Ancients were utter Strangers. If we come to Particulars, who of the Ancients ever unraveled the Chronology of the Old Testament, like Archbishop Usher, and Sir John Marsham? . . . Who has ever given so rational and so intelligible an Account of the Design and Intent of the several parts of the Ceremonial Law, as Dr. Spenser? Who has acquainted the World with the Geography of Genesis, or the Natural History of the Bible, like Monsieur Bochart? These are much harder Things than the lengthening of a fine-spun Allegory, or than a few moral Reflections, which constitute the greatest Part of the Ancient Comments.[37]

Wotton acknowledges that the "first fathers" understood the New Testament better than modern scholars. But with the split between synagogue and church, "the great number of Allusions to Jewish Customs and Traditions which are to be found in the New Testament" could no longer be understood naturally but only through careful study and reading. This knowledge, with few exceptions the ancients lacked, and they could not acquire the kind of expertise in "Eastern Antiquities" modern scholars presently attain.[38]

Wotton undoubtedly could have expanded his list of modern authorities to include Simon, le Clerc, Lightfoot, Selden, and his own favorite, Surenhusius, had he wanted to and had he written several decades later. But already by the end of the seventeenth century, he held a deep appreciation of the new scholarship in biblical studies of his generation, including the critical element of mastering "the Writings of the Rabbins and the Talmudists" and reading the New Testament in the light of the cultural data they provide. Most importantly, Wotton offered a remarkable self-consciousness that he was living in a unique age because of this new scholarship. The study of rabbinic literature by Christians had become an actual signal of modernity. Wotton fully comprehended that his era marked a special moment in the history of Christian scholarship, in Christian self-understanding, and in the growing awareness of the Jewish factor in Western civilization. In linking his discourse on modernity to his awareness that new linguistic and historical approaches had revolutionized the study of Christianity and Judaism, Wotton had underscored what was unique about his generation. He had also pointed to the novel ways in which each religion would define itself in the future by the standards and values implicit in the new scholarship, each individually but also in conversation with the other.

Conclusion

This book has attempted to identify and reconstruct a neglected chapter in intellectual history, in the history of scholarship, and in the evolution of Christian attitudes toward Judaism. It has argued that the crisis of historicism helped to precipitate a more tolerant attitude toward rabbinic Judaism among certain Christian clerical circles. Historical and philological scholarship engendered a fundamental shift from invalidation and repulsion to validation and endorsement of rabbinic literature on the part of a growing number of Christian scholars. In a period of heightened uncertainty and anxiety about Christian origins, the rabbis could now be safely employed to explicate and confirm the foundations of the Christian faith. Far from being marginal to Anglo-Christian life, Judaism subsequently assumed a more central place in the theological-political debates of this era as a cultural resource to be entrusted with illuminating and reconfirming the theological foundations of Christianity and its sacred writings.

This was, of course, not the first time Christians had mastered Hebrew and Aramaic, examined the medieval exegetical tradition, and noticed the liturgical, homiletical, mystical, and political traditions of the Jews. Indeed, several generations of Christian Hebraists had produced a significant library of scholarly works that long proceeded this era.[1] In the previous century, especially in England, as we saw in the last chapter, polymaths such as Edward Pococke, John Lightfoot, and especially John Selden had established the field of Christian rabbinical study through their prodigious writings, lending it an air of legitimacy and significance. Despite the deep-seated ambivalence on the part of some of them in immersing themselves in traditions Christianity had routinely repudiated, they achieved a remarkable facility in reading rabbinic literature in search of a unique Christian perspective by which to scrutinize its content. Some have even argued that this scholarly interest on the part of Christians in Judaism was actually waning by the eighteenth century, that the intense interest in Judaism had given way to interest in other religions and cultures, and to a backlash of sorts, pushing Christian Hebraism to the margins of modern culture.[2]

It is my contention, based on the portrait I have tried to present in the previous chapters, that Christian Hebraism had not expired or even receded by the eighteenth century; it had simply transformed itself in a novel way. The thinkers I have described in this book were not interested in Judaism merely as an aspect of their antiquarian scholarship, or out of a primary intellectual engagement with the past, or even as a personal quest to better understand their origins. They were driven to study Judaism, especially rabbinic literature and culture, because their own identity as Christians urgently required it. Historical scholarship had denuded the positive markers of what Christianity had always meant; it had obscured the teachings of Jesus and the Apostles, had called into question the very authority of sacred Scripture, and had eroded the very links from which the New Testament legitimized its teaching in relation to the Hebrew Bible. A Christian identity in crisis engendered by the corrosive forces of scholarly criticism was in search of new ways to understand its past and to overcome the dilemma of its present lack of confidence. The study of ancient Judaism in the eighteenth century was not only a natural and organic part of an explosion of knowledge in the form of books, pamphlets, and essays that the new scholarship had spawned. It was a way to reinvent the Christian past, to reinvigorate Christian identity, and to buttress the New Testament against the accusations that its truths were inauthentic and suspect. Through rabbinic Judaism, Christians could rediscover their true selves.

The eighteenth-century Christian students of rabbinic literature were different from Selden, Lightfoot, or Pococke in yet another dramatic way. While these seventeenth-century polymaths were profoundly learned in rabbinic Judaism and had elevated the study of the rabbis to a position unprecedented in the history of Christian exegesis, their scholarship was exclusively in Latin and it remained in the domain of a very elite world of learning. In contrast, their successors in the next century began to bring these findings to a much broader public audience. By choosing to publish their work in the vernacular as well as in Latin, they concluded that the wisdom of the rabbis was never pernicious or dangerous to a larger community of readers, clergy and laity alike. By translating actual rabbinic texts into English, especially the Mishnah, they opted to disseminate as widely as possible rabbinic attitudes and practices rather than limit their accessibility to a small coterie of learned scholars.

In order to demonstrate these claims and to construct a vivid portrait of Christian engagement with Judaism in early eighteenth-century England, I began with the life and writings of the convert Moses Marcus as my entry point and initial guide. His internal struggle between his former religious self and his new one, his attempts to ingratiate himself among Christian theologians and church leaders, and his embrace of the causes of religious orthodoxy along with his emerging pride as an expert in Hebrew and as expositor of Judaism have allowed us to visualize a fascinating personal odyssey as well as a wider segment of elite Christian society with which Marcus had contact, clergy such as David Wilkins, Daniel Waterland, Zachary Pearce, Johann Gottlob Carpzov, Edward Chandler, and others.

But Marcus's quest to retain a part of his Jewish self while proudly affirming his new Christian faith seems to have imploded at the same time he suffered severe economic decline and professional failure. Marcus imagined that his linguistic skills and his intimate knowledge of Jewish sources would make him attractive to the Christian intellectual elite of London. Indeed, his decision to affiliate with the Anglican Church while offering his services as an expert in Judaism seems to have initially impressed his mentor David Wilkins and several other patrons who willingly supported his pedagogic and publishing ventures. But Marcus struggled to hold his own economically and intellectually in the circles of Christian clergy who he believed would appreciate and seek out his knowledge and insight and reward him accordingly. In the final analysis, Marcus was neither a deep religious thinker nor a profound reader of rabbinic texts. His conventional knowledge was soon replicated and even surpassed by a growing number of Christian scholars of Judaism. His mediation between Judaism and Christianity, as a defender of the integrity of the Hebrew Scripture and as an interpreter of the Judaic faith and praxis to his new co-religionists, proved to be no longer critical to them. Their intense Jewish interests could be pursued without his agency as they gained direct access to the sources of Jewish literature.

More significantly, Marcus's perspective on post-biblical Judaism, on rabbinic law and theology, and on the historical and spiritual relations between Judaism and Christianity was sorely circumscribed by the limitations of his own education in Judaism and by the constraints of his newly discovered faith, which proclaimed that to be a Christian ultimately meant to repudiate one's belief in rabbinic Judaism. Marcus could align himself with Christian theologians who sought to protect the Hebrew Bible from the onslaughts of those critics who questioned its authenticity as the record of divine revelation. His defense of the Hebrew Bible and his testimony that Jews faithfully transmitted it from generation to generation did not contradict his posture that the new covenant of the church had superseded the old one of the rabbis. His passage from Judaism to Christianity as a young adult, equipped with the ordinary skills of a yeshivah student but no more, indelibly shaped the impression of Judaism he articulated in all of his extant writings. He could not offer a deeper or more nuanced representation of his ancestral heritage than that which he had learned as a child and that which he had been instructed to repudiate as an adolescent. He had personally crossed the boundary from Judaism to Christianity; he had challenged publicly the authority of London's leading rabbi; and despite his misgivings on abandoning his family and community, he had firmly repudiated rabbinic Judaism by affirming his new Christian identity. He could willingly defend the Jewish Bible, but he could not show support for and certainly could not champion the study of rabbinic Judaism for the Christian community.

Yet, ironically, members of the constituency Marcus tried to serve wanted more than he could offer. Inspired by Surenhusius and before him the seventeenth-century pioneers in the study of the rabbis, several Christian scholars took a step Marcus was incapable of taking: they assiduously studied rabbinic writings; they utilized them to probe the foundations of Christianity; and they underscored the importance of post-biblical Jewish learning for the education of all Christian clerics, indeed, for all Christians. Our story, which commenced with Marcus's attempt to define a liminal intellectual space for himself as "a converted Jew," ultimately closes with his failure to overcome the traditional polarities and stereotypes defining Christianity against Judaism. Boundary crossers such as Surenhusius, Michel de la Roche, Wotton, and Ockley were attempting to rethink and refashion the relationships between the two religions in new and bold ways. Marcus ultimately proved incapable of dislodging those rigid demarcations of the past.

I began this book with the aggressive comments of Humphrey Prideaux and Moses Marcus against the rabbis, their oral law, and the arguments of David Nieto, and I concluded with the prodigious efforts of Surenhusius, Wotton, and Ockley to utilize rabbinic sapience as a key in unlocking the truths of the Christian faith. In other words, even as Christians and Jews continued to play out their ancient theological debate, with each affirming the supremacy of their respective faiths, validating the one by invalidating the other, they were also beginning to approach each other in a new light. Nieto, Marcus, and Prideaux, despite their personal acquisition of considerable knowledge about and appreciation of the literatures of ancient Judaism and Christianity, continued to define themselves primarily though traditional categories. Surenhusius, Wotton, and Ockley were committed to exploring new ways of envisioning the historical and contemporary connections between the two faith communities.

The paradox of this fascinating moment in Jewish-Christian relations is that it transpired, more or less, without direct Jewish involvement. Nieto's presence hovered throughout, certainly as a target of Marcus's attempt to free himself of his Jewish past. But the remainder of our story took place exclusively within Christian circles. The conversation usually lacked actual Jewish interlocutors, although the Christian participants focused much of their attention on Judaism and rabbinic literature. Their preoccupation with Judaism was triggered by their own internal theological debates, by the new historical and textual scholarship, and by a seeming existential need to search for their Judeo-Christian roots. It had little to do with socially appreciating or even tolerating contemporary Jews or wishing to extend them greater political rights and privileges in English society. In the absence of real Jews with whom to converse, Christian readers of Jewish texts engaged with the Jewish past on the basis of their newly developed scholarly skills in understanding biblical and rabbinic sources and occasionally through the agency of former Jews such as Marcus. Ironically, a key spokesman and defender of Jewish interests in this narrative is a convert who was ambivalent about his identity but who was comfortable in the role of instructor of Judaism for Christians. When Jews were attacked as falsifiers of Holy Scripture, he saw himself as their protector. In examining his image as an advocate for Judaism within the clerical culture of eighteenth-century London, I have underscored the potential role of some converts in serving as conduits of culture between Judaism and Christianity, as agents of interfaith communication and dialogue between the two communities, and even as champions of the highest standards of scholarship in studying Hebraic texts. But I have also emphasized, as was exemplified by the case of Moses Marcus, the obvious limits in their abilities and the barriers in their life experiences that would not allow them to present Judaism fully and openly.

Many of the most significant cultural wars of this period are to be located in the religious polemics and debates among men of faith rather than between the secular and the religious aspects of society. The world of the faithful was hardly a disenchanted one, ready to excise religion at its core. Theology was transformed by libraries, printing presses, and coffee houses, but it remained a potent force in the cultural politics of the day. Moreover, the origins of historical scholarship can also be situated within the same matrix of the struggles of religious and political identity that dominated this era. More sophisticated than ever before and more advanced in its linguistic and literary tools of analysis, historical scholarship remained wedded to theological discussion and focused on religious history to a considerable degree. This revision of the narrative of previous scholarship, one of offering an alternative to the triumphant march of secularism and historicism, certainly calls into question the meaning of modernity as it applies to the cultural world of England in the early eighteenth century.[3]

I ended the last chapter by pointing to a connection made by William Wotton himself in his discourse on the wisdom of the moderns versus the ancients. In their new mastery of Hebrew subjects, in their use of unprecedented linguistic and historical tools, and in their recently discovered appreciation of rabbinic literature as a powerful resource for penetrating the meaning of the New Testament, the moderns had surely proven themselves superior to their ancient counterparts in actually understanding more broadly and more profoundly the origins of their own faith. The new scholarship, even as Wotton recorded it at an early stage of its accomplishments, at the close of the seventeenth century, had allowed Christians to know more about their past than in any previous age.

Wotton, of course, was speaking exclusively about scholarly advances in weighing the advantages of his own generation over previous ones. One wonders if his elegant paean to the moderns might signal even more profoundly an unmistakable recognition that these new studies and their revolutionary impact were part of a larger reevaluation of the place of Judaism in Western culture and if they might at least offer the promise of the most radical restructuring yet of the relationships between the Christian and Jewish faiths as they viewed each other in a different light. Accompanying the dynamic political culture of England, where theology and piety were still of utmost importance and where historical criticism could affirm religious ideologies as it confused and destabilized them, was this prominent elevation of Judaism as a cultural resource for Christianity.

Whether Judaism and its sources would continue to fascinate Christian scholars and religious leaders in subsequent years or would simply recede again to the margins of culture, losing the élan it had appeared to gain in this unique era, is beside the point. Wotton apparently understood something about his own generation that we have generally disregarded, that in accentuating the significance of the Christian discovery of Judaism in his lifetime, he had identified a vital ingredient of what was "modern" about his own era. To our own generation, which has witnessed the unprecedented blossoming of Judaic studies at universities and seminaries around the world, pursued at the highest level by Jews and Christians alike, his insight is especially meaningful.

The Dutch Edition of Moses Marcus's Conversionary Treatise

During the period Moses Marcus lived in Amsterdam, immediately after *The Principal Motives* had been published in 1724, it is likely he was introduced to Jacob Campo Weyerman (1677–1747), the colorful author, journalist, and publisher. They also could have met in London since Weyerman often visited there. He learned of Marcus's recent work and decided to translate it and publish it in Dutch with certain embellishments. The book was published some years later in Amsterdam without a publication date.[1] Who was this Weyerman and what motivated him to take on such a project in the first place?

Jacob Weyerman, after a short stint in the military, worked as a painter and then an art dealer and traveled through much of Europe. By 1720, he had lived in several southern Dutch towns, where he became a writer and a publisher of weekly newspapers including the *Amsterdamsche Hermes* (1721–23), *Ontleeder der Gebreeken* (1723–25), and the *Vrolyken Tuchtheer* (1729–30). He also published poetry, biography, and pamphlets. His most famous work was a four-volume study of the lives of Dutch painters.

Weyerman was known for his caustic wit, which sometimes got him into trouble, even landing him in jail. He poked fun at all kinds of people, including women, Catholics, Germans, and especially the authorities. As a youth, he studied ancient history, theology, and ancient languages, including some Hebrew. His periodicals reveal a specific Dutch style of outrageous satire. He was fascinated in relating the adventures of alchemists, Rosicrucians, freemasons, and Hermeticists. He tantalized his readership with discussions of freethinkers and libertines, both Dutchmen and foreigners such as Toland, Hobbes, Spinoza, and Vanini. He was even accused of being an atheist and freemason himself. He generally ignored doctrine except in his mocking history of popery.

His consistent ridicule of almost every subject he touched made him less an ideologue and more an iconoclast interested in laying bare all superstition and ignorance, no matter what the source. He was also a publicist of the new sciences, denigrating medical quacks and endless theorizing. He applauded empirical investigation based on lucid speculation and highlighted such contemporary scientists as Willis, Digby, and the Van Helmonts. His most charming quality was his ability to depict real people and real life. Patricians, booksellers, theologians, and prostitutes all found a place in his journals, and he relished the opportunity to sneer at and poke fun at them all.[2]

This also seems to be the spirit in which he approached the translation of Marcus's work, hardly an entertaining or amusing book in its original version. To publish it in Dutch, in the familiar Weyerman style required considerable touching up. This he did by eliminating specific details irrelevant to his readers and by removing Marcus's redundancies. Here was an opportunity not so much to denigrate rabbinic Judaism but rather to poke fun at it. He accomplished this by inserting Dutch expressions of a colorful nature, transforming a dull account into a lively one. So rabbis were described as lying like common lawyers, sitting with their glasses in hand discussing the name of the Messiah, or turning red with shame like the color of cut watermelons.

What was missing from Marcus's work were some good stories, some rabbinic fairy tales that would comically highlight the nature of rabbinic culture as Weyerman imagined it. These he found in the famous *Maaseh-Buch,* translated into German and published in Amsterdam in 1723. Choosing carefully from its fifty-four stories, he selected several rabbinic novellas, which he peppered with Dutch stylistic extravagances to bring out their comic flavor, as a kind of Jewish version of Mother Goose.

P. J. Buijnsters, the only scholar to have studied this work systematically, argues that Weyerman's satire is more playful than nasty, more entertaining than hateful. Despite his crude language about Ashkenazic Jews and talmudic masters, he never objected to the right of Jews to live freely in the Dutch Republic. He treated Judaism as he treated other cultures and religions, especially Catholicism, which fostered, to his mind, too much superstition and ignorance. He expressed ambivalence similar to other critics of the Enlightenment era in advocating the protection of Jewish citizens while ridiculing the seemingly irrational aspects of their religious life.[3]

It is unclear how his readers responded to his radical emendations to Marcus's volume, whether or not they saw them in the same vein as his other satiric works. It is also unclear why, of all books, he chose Marcus's unspectacular and modest publication, if his ultimate aim was to satirize the rabbis rather than to engage in a theological discussion with them about the oral law. And Marcus's declarations of Anglican Christian piety would have seemed highly inappropriate to an alleged free-thinking atheist who acknowledged no creed at all. Perhaps Marcus's quasi-celebrity status as a rich man's son who had disavowed his birthright made the account of his conversation a story to be told to Dutch readers, at least in the padded version Weyerman ultimately produced. One might assume that neither Marcus nor his Anglican sponsors were allowed any editorial control over Weyerman's publication. It is also likely that they were most unhappy with the final result.

Constructing a Genealogy of a Christian Scholarly Discipline: William Wotton's History of Christian Writers on the Legal Writings of the Jews

I have reproduced here the first chapter of Wotton's *Miscellaneous Discourses* (London, 1718), pp. 1–9, with my annotation, to illustrate the author's genuine need to demonstrate that his scholarly efforts were not merely those of an isolated individual but were part of the collective labors of a larger academic community that had emerged several generations earlier. To my knowledge, Wotton's history of the Christian study of rabbinic texts, primarily the Mishnah and Maimonides' *Mishneh Torah,* represents one of the earliest attempts to present a history of Christian scholarship on classical Jewish texts. As such, it served to promote the author's own accomplishments and those of his contemporaries as the pinnacle and culmination of an intellectual project that had already been pursued by a long line of accomplished Hebraists for well over 150 years.

Wotton's primary interest in the study of Judaism revolved around halakhic texts, those that allowed Christian scholars to understand the legal thinking of Jews. For him, this was a critical part of understanding the culture surrounding the New Testament and early Christianity. He acknowledged and appreciated the earlier work of Christians who had focused primarily on the ethical teachings of Judaism, such as that found in the *Pirke Avot,* but he considered the explication of legal materials a significant advance beyond these preliminary studies in penetrating the essence of rabbinic culture.

Wotton's list of his professional ancestors who had assiduously studied the Mishnah and Gemarah was heavily weighted in favor of English scholars; Pococke, Selden, and Lightfoot received their due as the most important pioneers in the study of rabbinics for Christian purposes. But

Wotton was also quite familiar with their Dutch and German counter-parts, especially Cocceius and L'Empereur and the generation of their students who came after them. He clearly viewed the publication of the entire Mishnah by Surenhusius as the culmination of a long period of painstaking scholarship on the study of the Mishnah and recognized both here and throughout his writing the singular importance of this profes-sor from Amsterdam and his crowning achievement in completing a task of several generations. It would also be fair to say that Wotton's English translation and that of others inaugurated for him a further stage of Christian scholarship, one critical in disseminating the knowledge of rab-binic law to a new generation of scholars and laypersons alike and its sig-nificance in understanding early as well as contemporary Christianity.

By including the history of Maimonidean scholarship in his account, at least that focused on the study of the *Mishneh Torah*, Wotton also acknowl-edged its importance as an ancillary field of rabbinic study, given the prominent place this code has played in the development of Jewish law and how well it summarizes with elegant simplicity the core of talmudic arguments. He remained frustrated, however, by the progress of this schol-arship, for two reasons. It was not finished and too much of its exposition had avoided a consideration of the most legalistic sections of the rab-binic corpus, for Wotton "the hard-core" and most revealing part of the rabbinic mode of exegesis. He was also frustrated because Maimonidean scholarship, no matter how important it was, could not replace the study of the Mishnah and Gemarah in their own right. He reminded his read-ers at the end of this chapter that regardless of Maimonides' centrality for Jewish culture, his opinions are still not identical with normative rab-binic tradition. Maimonides' views are still only those of an individual interpreter and are thus equivalent to the pronouncements of important Catholic leaders and theologians in more contemporary times who speak forcefully on behalf of the Church but do not actually speak for the col-lective will of the Church itself.

By highlighting this chapter at the beginning of his work, as well as including at the end a complete list of all of those who had labored to translate the Mishnah over more than a century, Wotton had contextu-alized his own work within the framework of history. Not only could his scholarly efforts claim a noble historical pedigree, they also represented the apogee of a development that demonstrated the superiority of Chris-tian scholarship in recent times. In Wotton's age, Christian learning had reached such heights that it could even penetrate the esoteric and in-accessible writings of the rabbis. It could even accomplish this feat with-out the agency of Jewish teachers and translators. Christians were for the first time independently capable of knowing intimately the Jewish mind and appropriating its insights in understanding themselves. Wotton's documentation of Christian scholars of rabbinics was thus an acknowl-edgment of his indebtedness to those who had worked tirelessly before him to reach this point, a celebration of the recent Christian triumph in mastering the one field that had eluded their ancestors, and the expec-tation of the rich rewards this accomplishment would entail for the entire Christian world.

[1] Of Christian Writers who have publish'd and commented upon any Titles of the Traditional Laws of the Jews.

It may seem very wonderful, since the Constitutions and Traditions of the Elders[1] are so often appeal'd to, and so often, as well as so justly blamed by our blessed Saviour in his Discourses with the Jews, which are preserv'd to us in the Writings of the Evangelists, that the generality of learned Men who have appeared in such Numbers since the [2] Restoration of Letters, have known so little of them, as it is plain by their Writings that they did. For tho' here and there an inquisitive Man among the Christians had look'd into those Writings of the Jews, in which these Traditions have carefully been preserv'd; yet their Number has been very small, and for want of Translations of the Original Books themselves, to which other Men might appeal, what these Men said had not its due Weight. Learning had been propagated in Europe for above 150 Years, and the great Writers among the ancient Greeks and Romans, both Christian and Pagan printed, and most of the Grecian Authors translated into Latin, which is the common Language of the Learned in these Parts of the World, before any one ritual Title of the old gen-uine Traditions of the Jews had been publish'd among us.[2] Paulus Fagius indeed, soon after the Reformation, set forth the *Pirke Avoth,* in which we have a concise History of the Propagation of Tradition among the Jews, with some few Apoph-thegms of the first Doctors from whom they reckon their Traditions.[3] But then that Title had little Ritual in it; for that wherein the Traditions of the Elders consisted was not much better known. In the Year 1629, Johannes Cocceius of Bremen, printed two Misnic Titles *Sanhedrin* and *Maccoth,* in Hebrew and Latin in Amsterdam, which contain an authentic Account of the Jewish Courts of Jus-tice, of their Method of animadverting upon Offenders, with judicious Notes, and large and valuable Excerpta out of the Babylonia *Gemara* (which is properly called the *Talmud*) upon those two Titles.[4] Constantin L'Empereur printed the Title *Middoth,* in which we have the Dimensions of the Temple and all its Parts in 1630; and the Title *Babba Kama,* which treats of Damages done by Beasts, and Fire, and Pits, and Things of the like Nature, specify'd in Exodus xxi, in 1637. He had finish'd [3] several other Titles for the Press, but whether they were ever printed I know not. L'Empereur was admirably well vers'd in the Jewish Learn-ing, and by his great Skill in the Civil Law, with which (tho' he did not profess it) he was well acquainted; he was enabled to compare the Decisions of the Talmud-ists with the Constitutions of the Roman Law-givers as he has done throughout the whole Title. Besides this, he publish'd a Jewish Tract call'd *Halicoth Olam,* in which the Ways of Reasonings of these Matters are accurately explain'd; and which, well understood, are they promise to be, a Key to those Studies.[5]

Mr. Robert Sheringham, Fellow of Caius College in Cambridge, and a very great Honour to the University in his Time, printed the Title *Joma,* or of the great Expiation, in Hebrew and Latin, with a learned Commentary, at London in 1648, when he was ejected for his Loyalty, for which he was long an Exile abroad.[6] Some

Years after Dr. Pocock, who truly [is] an Honour to his Age and Countrey, printed several of Maimonides's Prefaces to this Commentaries upon the *Misna*[7] in Arabic and Latin, under the Title of *Porta Mosis* at Oxford in 1655; in which as the Title promises, a Gate is opened to the understanding of the whole Traditional Law of the Jews.[8] After him Mr. William Guise, late Fellow of All Souls College in Oxford, (Who to the inestimable Loss of the whole Eastern Learning, was taken off in the Flower of his Years) attempted to translate the whole *Misna* into Latin, but he finish'd only the six first Titles of the *Seder Zeraim*, which were printed after his Death at Oxford in 1690, by the late learned [4] Savilian Professor of Astronomy in that University, Dr. Edward Bernard.[9] Some few Titles more have been printed abroad within these late forty Years, among which the most considerable is Title *Sotah,* (or of the Woman accused of Adultery, who was to be try'd by the Waters of Jealousy) by Johannes Christophorus Wagenseilius; to which he has added a noble Commentary, in which he had taught his Christian Readers abundance of Things concerning the Jewish Affairs, very well worth knowing; besides what immediately related to the Title which he undertook to illustrate. He also, as Cocceius had done before him, annex'd large Excerpta out of the *Gemara* to the Text of the *Misna.*[10] Sebastianus Schmidius publish'd the Titles *Shabbath* and *Eruvin* (which the Reader will see here in English) with the Commentary of Maimonides and Bartenora.[11] Houtingius also and Lundius have given us the Titles *Rosh Hashana,* (i.e. of the Feast of Trumpets, or the Beginning of the Year) and *Taanith* (i.e. of the Jewish Fasts) which they have illustrated with large and useful Commentaries.[12]

All this did not contain a full third part of the *Misna*; and all this while the Original Text of the Pharisaic Law was unknown to most Men. Mr. Selden indeed, who was a great Master of the whole Talmudic Learning, has give us just Discourses upon many different Subjects, in which he largely and fully explained the Opinions of these ancient Doctors upon those Heads which he treats of.[13] And Dr. Lightfoot, a Man no ways his Inferior in that Sort of Knowledge, has apply'd it with great Advantage to the Illustration of the Biblical Text, and thereby [5] cleared abundance of Things in the New Testament, which were before unknown to the learnedest Interpreters of the Scriptures among the Christians.[14]

At last Gulielmus Surenhusius, now Professor of Hebrew and Greek in which they call the Schola Illustris at Amsterdam, undertook to give us the *Misna* entire in Hebrew and Latin, with the Commentaries of Maimonides and Bartenora at large upon the whole Work. This he publish'd in Amsterdam in six Folio's, of which the first Volume was printed in 1698, and the last in 1703. So lately is it that that Book which the most considerable part of the Jewish Nation esteems as the authentic Text of their Oral Law, as it has done for near 1600 Years past, has been entirely communicated to the Christian World. The greatness of the Undertaking deterr'd other Men, which makes our Obligation to him so much the greater.[15]

The Jews indeed have had for several Ages, full and plain Institutions of the whole Oral Law among them, written in a clear intelligible Style. The chiefest of these is the *Yad hachazaca* (i.e. the strong hand) of Maimonides; in which in an easy and methodical Manner, and in a clear Style, he has given his Countrymen an ample Account of the whole Talmudic Law. This has been printed several times among the Jews, and has been from the time of its first Publication valued by them as it justly deserves.[16] And yet it is not much above 100 Years since its true Value has been much known to the learned Men among us. Petrus Cunaeus was one of the first that discover'd its great Usefulness, in his incomparable little

Book of the Commonwealth of the Jews.[17] Joseph Scaliger, before him, knew the worth of that great Man, and of his *More Nevochim,* which he commends according to its Merit in several places of his Epistles, but that Book is not ritual; however Joseph Scaliger did not stop there; he had read the [6] *Misna* carefully, as appears from many places of his Writings; but he publish'd nothing upon these Subjects. He, however it was, who whilst he lived in Holland, where he spent his latter Years, inspired the young Men of that Nation with a Love of the Eastern Learning, by shewing them its instrinsick worth; so that in Truth we owe to his Example and Authority in a great measure, all those noble Performances by which Cunaeus, L'Empereur, De Dieu, Erpenius (who died early) and after him Golius, and many others of that Age and Countrey acquir'd so just a Reputation to themselves, and were so useful to those that came after them; and yet very few Titles of that great Work of Maimonides's were publish'd in Latin till our Father's Memory.[18] Dionysius, Son to the great Gerard John Vossius, translated the Title of *Idolatry,* with a very useful Commentary.[19] Georgius Gentius publish'd his *Hilcoth Deuth,* or Moral Precepts in Hebrew and Latin in Amsterdam in 1640;[20] Johannes Vorstius also translated his *Foundations of the Law,* but neither that nor any other of his Versions of Hebrew Books, of which we have several, are much esteem'd by the learned.[21] The excellent Dean of Norwich Dr. Prideaux, to whom this Generation are not a little oblig'd for his *Connexion of the History of the Old and New Testament,* publish'd two Titles out of Maimonides's *Yad* of the Laws concerning the *Poor and Stranger,* and the *Gifts of the Poor* some time ago;[22] and the learned and worthy Professor of the Hebrew Language at Oxford Dr. Robert Clavering, has lately given us two other Titles of the *Study of the Law* and *of Repentance,* in Hebrew and Latin with very useful Notes; all which for the curiosity of the Matter, and the easiness of the Style, are very proper to be put into the Hands of young Beginners.[23]

[7] But in all these Titles there is little Ritual, so that tho' these Pieces have their just and true Value; yet they do not much contribute towards understanding the Traditions of the Elders, of which we have an entire System in that admirable Work.[24] About forty Years ago Monsieur Colbert, that great Patron of Letters under the late King of France, employed Monsieur Lewis de Veil a Convert Jew, who was Master of a beautiful Latin Style, to turn the whole *Yad* into Latin. He printed some few Titles out of it in Latin, especially concerning the Temple Service, and the Method of Intercalations of the Jewish Year at Paris, when turning Protestant he came into England about the Year 1680, where he went on with that Work, and publish'd the Title of *Sacrifices* in the Year 1683 in London, with Abarbinel's Preface to his Commentaries upon Leviticus. It is a pity that he did not find Encouragement to go on with his Design, for tho' (as I heard some very great Judges in those Matters complain) he too often suffers his Latinity to get the better of his Hebrew; yet that Work, if he had gone thro' with it, would have been a noble and a pleasant Introduction to those who would willingly know these Things at an easy rate, and are often disgusted at the uncouthness and barbarity of the Style of most Writers upon these Subjects.[25] And lately Andreas Christophorus Zellerus has printed his Title *of the Red Heifer* at Amsterdam in 1711.[26] But all this and what else, has been publish'd by Christians out of those Pandects is very little in Comparison of the whole Work. And, after all, if we had it entire in Latin or [8] English, yet it wants a great deal of the Authority of the *Misna* itself, especially in contested Cases.

For we ought to consider that Maimonides lived in the Twelfth Century several Ages after the Talmud was sealed up (which it was upon the finishing of the

Babylonian *Gemara*) after the great Schools which the Jews kept for many Ages in Babylonia were destroy'd by the Saracenic Caliphs. The Jews were then dispers'd into Europe; and in Spain, in France, and England, they made numerous Settlements. At Corduba in Spain, Maimonides was born; there he began to compose his first great Work, which was his Commentaries upon the *Misna,* which he wrote in Arabic, the Language of the Morisco's and Arabs, among whom he had his Education. It was afterwards turn'd into Hebrew, and Dr. Pocock has given us a History of that Version in his Preface to the *Porta Mosis.* From that Version it is now publish'd in Latin by Surenhusius. That Commentary is drawn from the *Gemara*'s and the other ancienest Ritual Authors among the Jews. But still whatsoever Praise he may and does deserve, as an exact, intelligible and judicious Interpreter, who has cleared the whole Body of those Traditional Laws from the vast Load of impertinent and fabulous Stuff with, and under which it had so long lain mixed and opprest, he can be consider'd only as an Interpreter. Nothing that he says can be appealed to as a Record, when any essential Doubts arise.[27]

The Case is the same with him, (who ought to be placed in the Front of the Talmudic Commentators and Systematical Men,) and Solomon Jarchi [= Rashi] and Bartenora, when the meaning of any Decision is enquir'd after, as is with Stapleton, Bellarmin, or Du Perron, or any eminent Polemical Divines among the Papists.[28] They are readily allow'd by their own side to be good and useful Writers upon any Question that is controverted between us and the Church of Rome. But if any Man of that Communion should in the Heat of [9] Disputation be prest with the Authority of any of these Authors, by one of our Writers, who may judge that what they say is to his purpose; such a Man would instantly reply these were but single Doctors, they might err, and they very often do. We are not bound to stand to their Decisions. What says the Council of Trent? What says the Catechismus ad Parochos [that is, the catechism of the Council of Trent]? Is there any such thing in our establish'd Liturgies? So here, if a Question should arise relating to any material Constitution, either concerning its Sense or its Validity, no learned Jew will be determin'd by what Maimonides, or what Solomon Jarchi says, if it should seem to contradict the Text of the *Misna*; and much more if it cannot be reconcil'd to the settled Explications of the Text in the *Gemara*'s, especially that of Babylon which is of the greatest Authority. And now that the value of this Body of Laws, out of which I have printed two entire Titles, may be the better known by those of my Readers who are unacquainted with these Things (for as for others, if any such shall think it worth their while to look into these Papers, I do not pretend to teach them, but shall be very well contented if they shall think that I have not committed any great mistakes,) I shall say something concerning the Nature and Authority of these Misnic Laws, and the Uses that may be made of them by a Christian, either him that has any Commerce with Jews, or him that only desires to be thoroughly skill'd in the Doctrine of the Gospel of Jesus Christ, as it is deliver'd to us in the New Testament.

Notes

Introduction

1. A sampling of the vast literature on this subject would begin with Gershom Scholem, *Sabbatai Sevi: The Mystical Messiah* (Princeton, N.J., 1973); Yehudah Liebes, *Sod ha-Emunah Ha-Shabta'it: Koveẓ Ma'amarim* (Jerusalem, 1995); Yaakov Barnai, *Ha-Tenu'ah ha-Shabta'it: Hebetim Ḥevratiyim* (Jerusalem, 2000); and Rachel Elior, ed., *Ha-Ḥalom ve-Shivro: Ha-Tenu'ah Ha-Shabta'it u-Sheluḥoteha: Meshiḥiyut, Shabta'ut u-Frankizm,* 2 vols. (Jerusalem, 2001).

2. See, for example, Yosef Kaplan, *An Alternative Path to Modernity: The Sephardic Diaspora in Western Europe* (Leiden, 2000); Jonathan Israel, *The Radical Enlightenment: Philosophy and the Making of Modernity 1650–1750* (Oxford, 2001); Yirmiyahu Yovel, *Spinoza and Other Heretics,* 2 vols. (Princeton, N.J., 1989); Stephen Nadler, *Spinoza's Heresy: Immortality and the Jewish Mind* (Oxford, 2001).

3. See, for example, Adam Sutcliffe, *Judaism and Enlightenment* (Cambridge, 2003).

4. Gershon Hundert, *Jews in Poland-Lithuania in the Eighteenth Century: A Genealogy of Modernity* (Berkeley, 2004).

5. Yaron Ben Naeh, *Yehudim be-Mamlekhet ha-Sultanim: Ha Ḥevra ha-Yehudit ba-Impiri'ah ha-Otomanit be-Ma'ah ha-Shevah Esre* (Jerusalem, 2006).

6. Shmuel Feiner, *The Jewish Enlightenment* (Philadelphia, 2004); David Sorkin, *The Berlin Haskalah and German Religious Thought: Orphans of Knowledge* (London, 2000).

7. On her, see, for example, Natalie Z. Davis, *Women on the Margins: Three Seventeenth-Century Lives* (Cambridge, Mass., 1995), but especially the new critical edition of her diary with Hebrew translation and copious annotation, Chava Turniansky, ed., *Glikl: Zikhronot 1691–1719* (Jerusalem, 2006).

8. I first became acquainted with the life of Moses Marcus by my reading of Elisheva Carlebach's fascinating *Divided Souls: Converts from Judaism in Germany 1600–1750* (New Haven, Conn., 2001) and by the succinct account of his career in David Katz, *The Jews in the History of England 1485–1850)* (Oxford, 1994), pp. 206–15. Marcus's conversion is only one prominent example of a much larger phenomenon within both the Jewish and non-Jewish worlds. I have not primarily used Marcus's narrative, as Carlebach does, to study conversion in early modern Europe; rather, I use it mostly as a means of identifying and understanding the clerical circles with which Marcus had contact and their interest in rabbinic Judaism. What interests me primarily is his mingled Jewish-Christian identity and

his conspicuous role as a teacher of Judaism in a Christian world. On the subject of Jewish conversions to Christianity (excluding the wider phenomenon of the *converso*), besides Carlebach's work, see Todd Endelman, *Radical Assimilation in English Jewish History, 1656–1945* (Bloomington, Ind., 1990); Todd Endelman, ed., *Jewish Apostasy in the Modern World* (New York and London, 1987); and Michael Ragussis, *Figures of Conversion: "The Jewish Question" and English National Identity* (Durham, N.C., 1995). On the general subject of conversion between Protestantism and Catholicism and between Christianity and Islam in Europe and in England in particular, the scholarly literature is vast. See, for example, Lewis Rambo, *Understanding Religious Conversion* (New Haven, Conn. and London, 1993); Robert W. Hefner, ed., *Conversion to Christianity: Historical and Anthropological Perspectives on a Great Transformation* (Berkeley and Los Angeles, 1993); Michael C. Questier, *Conversion, Politics and Religion in England, 1580–1625* (Cambridge, 1996); and Gauri Viswanathan, *Outside the Fold: Conversion, Modernity, and Belief* (Princeton, N.J., 1998). On two prominent eighteenth-century converts in English society, see Robert DeMaria, jun., "Psalmanazar, George (1679–1763)," *Oxford Dictionary of National Biography* (Oxford, 2004), http://www.oxforddnb.com/view/article/22858; and Anita McConnell, "Pitts, Joseph (1663?–1739?)," *Oxford Dictionary of National Biography.* http://www.oxforddnb.com/view/article/22345.

9. David B. Ruderman, *Jewish Thought and Scientific Discovery in Early Modern Europe* (New Haven, Conn., 1995; Detroit, Mich., 2001), chap. 11, pp. 310–31. See also Jacob Petuchowski, *The Theology of Haham David Nieto: An Eighteenth-Century Defense of the Jewish Tradition* (New York, 1954).

10. In addition to the bibliography listed above in notes 1 and 2, see especially Shalom Rosenberg, "Emunat Hakhamim," in Bernard Septimus and Isadore Twersky, eds., *Jewish Thought in the Seventeenth Century* (Cambridge, Mass., 1987), pp. 285–341.

11. Justin Champion, *The Pillars of Priesthood Shaken: The Church of England and Its Enemies 1660–1739* (Cambridge, 1992); idem, *Republican Learning: John Toland and the Crisis of Christian Culture 1696–1722* (Manchester and New York, 2003); idem, Introduction to John Toland, *Nazarenus* (Oxford, 1999); idem, "'To Know the Edition': Erudition and Polemic in Eighteenth-Century Clerical Culture,'" in Muriel McCarthy and Ann Simmons, eds., *The Making of Marsh's Library: Learning, Religion and Politics in Ireland 1650–1750* (Dublin, 2004), pp. 117–45; idem, "Apocrypha, Canon, and Criticism from Samuel Fisher to John Toland 1660–1718," in Allison Coudert, Sarah Hutton, Richard Popkin, and Gordon Weiner, eds., *Judaeo-Christian Intellectual Culture in the Seventeenth Century: A Celebration of the Library of Narcissus Marsh (1638–1713)* (Boston, 1999), pp. 91–117.

Most recently, Jonathan Sheehan, in *The Enlightenment Bible: Translation, Scholarship, Culture* (Princeton, N.J., 2005), arrives at a similar conclusion in seeing the early eighteenth century as a turning point regarding the authority of the Bible, especially in England. In Sheehan's words: "Whether in the hands of iconoclastic Catholics like the Oratorian scholar Richard Simon; radical philosophers like Baruch Spinoza, Thomas Hobbes, or Pierre Bayle; mainstream critics like Jean le Clerc; or religious radicals like Johann Heinrich Reitz, the foundations of the traditional biblical text became shaky and uncertain" (p. 27). In light of the threat of "an unfettered historical criticism" (pp. 33, 42), the Bible "hungered for a new stability" (p. 27).

Chapter 1

1. The standard work on Nieto is Petuchowski, *The Theology of Haham David Nieto*. See also Israel Solomons, *David Nieto: Haham of the Spanish and Portuguese Jews, Congregation Kahal Kadosh Sahar Asamim* (London, 1931). For additional bibliography, see Ruderman, *Jewish Thought and Scientific Discovery*, p. 310, n. 1. The full Spanish title of Nieto's book is *Mateh Dan y segunda parte del Cuzari: donde se prueva con razones naturales, irefragables demonstraciones, y reales consequencias la verdad dela ley mental, recebida por nuestros sabios autores de la Misna y Guemara* (London, 1714).

2. Compare Yosef Kaplan's important essay, "'Karaites' in the Early Eighteenth Century," in his *Alternative Path to Modernity*, pp. 234–79.

3. I cite from the modern Hebrew edition of *Ha-Kuzari ha-Sheni*, ed. Cecil Roth (Jerusalem, 1958), p. 3.

4. David Nieto, *Esh Dat* (London, 1715).

5. He composed a response, clarifying that he was not a Spinozist, entitled *De la divina providencia: O sea naturaleza universal, o natura naturante, tratado theologico* (London, 1704).

6. See Ruderman, *Jewish Thought and Scientific Discovery*, chap. 11, pp. 310–31.

7. Solomons reviews this evidence in his *David Nieto,* especially his correspondence with Dr. John Covel, the master of Christ's College, Cambridge.

8. Nieto, *Ha-Kuzari ha-Sheni,* viku'ah 1–3.

9. This is also well summarized in Petuchowski, *The Theology of Haham David Nieto,* chap. 6, pp. 69–74.

10. On Prideaux and his works, see Hugh de Quehen, "Prideaux, Humphrey," *Oxford Dictionary of National Biography* (Oxford, 2004), http://www.oxforddnb.com/view/article/22784; Peter M. Holt, "The Treatment of Arab History by Prideaux, Ockley, and Sale," in Bernard Lewis and Peter M. Holt, eds., *Historians of the Middle East* (London, 1962), pp. 290–302. See also Paolo Bernardini, "The Silent Retreat of the Fathers: Episodes in the Process of Re-appraisal of Jewish History and Culture in Eighteenth-Century England," in Sian Jones, Tony Kushner, and Sarah Pearce, eds., *Cultures of Ambivalence and Contempt: Studies in Jewish-Non-Jewish Relations, Essays in Honour of . . . James Parkes* (London, 1998), pp. 102–8.

11. Humphrey Prideaux, *The Old and the New Testament Connected in the History of the Jews and Neighboring Nations from the Declension of the Kingdoms of Israel and Judah to the Time of Christ,* part 1 (London, 1716), pp. xiii, xxiv, 49, 108, 136, 146, 152, 154, and passim.

12. Ibid., 1:322.

13. Ibid., 1:323.

14. Ibid., 1:323–26. On the long history of Christian arguments regarding the oral law, see Ḥain Merhaviah, *Ha-Talmud be-Rei ha-Naẓrut: Ha-Yaḥas le-Sifrut Yisrael shele'aḥar ha-Mikra be-Olam ha-Noẓri bi'mai ha-Beinayim* (Jerusalem, 1970).

15. Prideaux, *The Old and the New Testament,* part 2 (London, 1718), p. 549.

16. Thomas Morgan, *The Moral Philosopher in a Dialogue between Philatethes a Christian Deist and Theophanes a Christian Jew in Which the Grounds and Reasons of Religion in General and Particularly of Christianity, as Distinguished from the Religion of Nature [Are Discussed] . . .* (London, 1737), pp. 48–49. On Morgan, see Peter Harrison, *"Religion" and the Religions of the English Enlightenment* (Cambridge, 1990), index; and by the same author, "Morgan, Thomas (d. 1743)," *Oxford Dictionary of National Biography,* http://www.oxforddnb.com/view/article/19239.

17. The work was printed by "J. Humphreys for E. Bell at the Cross-Keys and Bible, in Cornhill; and Sold by J. Roberts, near the Oxford-Arms, in Warwick Lane" for two shillings. The same Roberts also printed and sold Marcus's *The Ceremonies of the Present Jews* five years later for the price of one shilling. James Roberts was a well-known London publisher who dealt mainly with pamphlets and periodicals. See the numerous references to him in David Foxon, *Pope and the Early Eighteenth-Century Book Trade,* rev. and ed. James McLaverty (Oxford, 1991), index.

18. Moses Marcus, *The Principal Motives and Circumstances That Induced Moses Marcus to Leave the Jewish, and Embrace the Christian Faith, with a Short Account of His Sufferings Thereupon* (London, 1724), p. 106.

19. Ibid., pp. 106–7.

20. Ibid., pp. 107–9.

21. Ibid., pp. 109–16; the citation is from p. 116.

Chapter 2

1. Alfred Feilchenfeld, *Denkwuerdigkeiten der Glückel von Hameln, aud dem jüdisch-deutschen uebersetz* (Berlin, 1923), pp. 326–27; George Simon, ed., *Genealogical Tables of Jewish Families: 14th–20th Centuries; Forgotten Fragments of the History of the Fraenkel Family by Louis and Henry Fraenkel* (Munich, 1999), unpaginated handwritten genealogical table. My thanks to Professor Chava Turniansky for these references. See also David Kaufmann, "Rabbi Zevi Ashkenazi and His Family in London," *Transactions of the Jewish Historical Society of England* 3:1896–98 (Edinburgh and London, 1898), pp. 102–25; Katz, *The Jews in the History of England,* pp. 206–15; R. J. D'Arcy Hart, "The Family of Mordecai Hamburger," *Miscellanies of the Jewish Historical Society of England 3* (London, 1937), pp. 57–76; Natalie Zemon Davis, *Women on the Margin,* pp. 246–47, 258–59.

2. Gedalia Yogev, *Diamonds and Coral: Anglo-Dutch Jews and Eighteenth-Century Trade* (New York, 1978), pp. 130, 149–59. On p. 303, he mentions the letters between Marcus Moses and Sir Richard Hoare found in the British Library, Papers of Thomas Pitt, add. mss. 22, 842–52. Additional information is found in Hart, "The Family of Mordecai Hamburger," especially pp. 59–63. In 1717, the Madras government entrusted Marcus Moses with the fashioning of a jewel for a lieutenant named John Roach. In 1718, Pierre Dulivier, his former associate, accused Marcus Moses in court of overcharging him, but Moses successfully defended himself against the accusation. Hart claims, on the basis of documents from the East India Company London office, that Marcus Moses returned to Fort St. George, India, as late as 1731, not earlier, as Yogev has suggested.

3. British Library Ms. Sloane 1968, ff. 53–56; Yogev, *Diamonds and Coral,* pp. 158–59.

4. The entire conflict is described by Kaufmann, "Rabbi Zevi Ashkenazi," and by Katz, *The Jews in the History of England,* pp. 206–13. Kaufmann mentions on p. 115 that the evangelical deacon Adam Andreas Cnollen of Fürth excerpted the details of Johanan Holleschau's book and published them in a periodical called *New Things and Old,* anno 114, 4th ser., 1:617, which I have not been able to locate. See also Cecil Roth, *History of the Great Synagogue of London 1690–1940* (London, 1950), pp. 29–40; R. Uri Phoebus Hamburger, *Urim ve-Tummin* (London, 1707); Johanan Holleschau, *Ma'aseh Rav* in *Teshuvat Ha-Geonim* (Amsterdam, 1707); Johann Jacob Schudt, *Jüdische Merckwürdigketen,* 4 vols. (Frankfurt and

Leipzig, 1715–18), vol. 4 (1718), pp. 135–37. On the *ḥerem* of the twelfth-century Rabenu Tam and its history in England, see G. W. Busse, "The Herem of Rabenu Tam in Queen Anne's London," *Transactions of the Jewish Historical Society of England* 21 (1968): 138–47.

5. Marcus, *The Principal Motives*, pp. xvi–xviii.

6. Ibid., pp. xviii–xix.

7. Ibid., pp. xix–xx.

8. Ibid., pp. xx–xxii.

9. Ibid., p. xxii.

10. Ibid., pp. xxiii–xiv.

11. For all the information on this subject, I am most indebted to Dr. Jutta Braden Hansenet of Hamburg, who is presently engaged in a major project on Jewish missionaries and converts in Hamburg in the seventeenth and eighteenth centuries. She kindly offered me her own speculations about the circumstances of Marcus's conversion in Hamburg and London, which I found most persuasive and have adopted here. She also provided me with an extensive bibliography on the subject, some of which I have consulted and mention in this note. On the merchant adventurers in Hamburg, see Maria Möring, "Die Englische Kirche in Hamburg und die Merchant Adventurers," in *Hamburgische und englische Kaufleute: Forschungen und Berichte aus dem Hanseatischen Lebensraum: Englandfahrt—Hamburgfahrt: Aus der Blütezeit des deutsch-englischen Handels zwischen 1400 und 1800 und vom Bau der englischen Kirche in Hamburg,* Hamburger Wirtschaftschronik 5 (Hamburg, 1975), pp. 29–60. On religious nonconformists in Hamburg during this time, see Michael D. Driedger, *Obedient Heretics: Mennonite Identities in Lutheran Hamburg and Altona during the Confessional Age,* St. Andrews Studies in Reformation History (Aldershot, 2002); and Walter Rustmeier, "Oliger Pauli oder der Plan einer Apostolischen Gemeinde zur Vereinigung der Juden und Christen in Altona," *Schriften des Vereins für Schleswig-Holsteinische Kirchengeschichte,* 2. Reihe (Beiträge und Mitteilungen) 19 (1963): 69–87. See also Joachim Whaley, *Religious Tolerance and Social Change in Hamburg* (Cambridge, 1985). On Esdras Edzard and his conversionary activity in Hamburg, see Carlebach, *Divided Souls,* pp. 81–83; Martin Friedrich, *Zwischen Abwehr und Bekehrung: Die Stellung der deutschen evangelishen Theologie zum Judentum im 17 Jahrhundert,* Beiträge zur historischen Theologie, 72 (Tübingen, 1988).

12. On the Jewish community and its rabbinic leadership in the area of Hamburg and Altona during the period Moses was studying there, see most recently Gabriele Zürn, *Die Altonaer Jüdische Gemeinde (1611–1873): Ritus und soziale Institutionen des Todes im Wandel* (Münster, 2001); Peter Freimark, "Das Obberrabbinat Altona-Hamburg-Wandsbek," in Arno Herzig and Saskia Rohde, eds., *Die Juden in Hamburg 1590–1990: Wissenschaftliche Beiträge der Universität Hamburg zur Ausstellung, Vierhundert Jahre Juden in Hamburg* (Hamburg, 1991), pp. 177–86, and in the same volume, Günter Marwedel, "Die ashkenasischen Juden im Hamburger Raum (bis 1780)," pp. 41–60. Again my thanks to Dr. Braden Hansenet for these references.

13. See Katz, *The Jews in the History of England,* pp. 190–95.

14. George Williams Sanders, ed., *Orders of the High Court of Chancery and Statutes of the Realm Related to Chancery from the Earliest Period to the Present Time* (London, 1845), 1:457–59.

15. Ibid., 1:458–59.

16. Ibid., 1:524–26. By the eighteenth century, Amsterdam was well known as a magnet for recent Jewish converts to Christianity who subsequently sought to

return to their ancestral faith, and it was thus an obvious destination for Moses to send his son for "rehabilitation." For other documented cases of such rehabilitation, see Elisheva Carlebach, "'Ich will dich nach Holland schicken . . .': Amsterdam and the Reversion to Judaism of German-Jewish Converts," in Martin Mulsow and Richard Popkin, eds., *Secret Conversions to Judaism in Early Modern Europe* (Leiden, 2004), pp. 51–69. My thanks to Matt Goldish for calling my attention to this essay.

17. Public Record Office, National Archives, Kew, Richmond, Orders of the Court of Chancery, C11/2790/21. The reference to swearing on the Hebrew Bible is found in C33/340 Lib. B. 1722 f.147a. Additional material regarding the suit is found in C33/348 B. 1726, f.98a; C33/350 B. 1727, f.255a; C33/350 B. 1727, f.306; C33/356 B. 1730, f.85b.

18. British Library, Ms. Lansdowne 988, f.374. The letter was printed by Cecil Roth in his *Anglo-Jewish Letters* (London, 1938), pp. 97–98.

19. Public Record Office, Orders of the Court of Chancery, C33/350 B.1727, f.255a; C33/350 B. 1727, f.306; C33/356 B. 1730, f.85b.

20. On this, see Appendix 1 below.

21. Marcus, *The Principal Motives,* page facing the title page.

22. Ibid., pp. viii–x.

23. Ibid., pp. xii–xiv.

24. On Wilkins, see Alastair Hamilton, "Wilkins, David (1685–1745)," in *Oxford Dictionary of National Biography,* http://www.oxforddnb.com/articles/29/29417; David C. Douglas, *English Scholars 1660–1730* (London, 1939, 1951), pp. 212–20; and Ms. Oxford Bodl. Mss. Eng.th.e.140, sermons, vol. 1, f.xiii–xix. There are many extant letters in manuscript written by Wilkins and received by him. Many were published in John Nichols, *Letters on Various Subjects, Literary, Political, and Ecclesiastical to and from William Nicolson D.D.* 2 vols., (London, 1809), 2, letters 185, 191–99, 204–8, 210, 213, 217–18, 220–21, 223, 225–26, 232, 245, 247–48, 250–51. The letters of Nicolson also include several to William Wotton and his replies, and they demonstrate his relations with Wilkins as well. On Wotton, see Chapter 5 below. There is also a letter from Wilkins in Maria Grazia and Mario Sina, eds., *Jean Le Clerc, Epistolario,* vol. 3 (1707–17) (Florence, 1994), p. 533, where Wilkins, in writing to le Clerc, sends his regards to William Surenhusius and asks forgiveness for not being in touch with him for a long time. On Surenhusius, see Chapter 4 below.

25. On Grabe, see Guenther Thomann, "John Ernst Grabe (1666–1711): Lutheran Syncretist and Anglican Patristic Scholar," *Journal of Ecclesiastical History* 43 (1992): 424–27.

26. The information in the last three paragraphs is gleaned from the references listed in the note 24.

27. David Wilkins, D.D, Prebendary of Canterbury and Chaplain to His Grace the Lord Archbishop of Canterbury, *A Sermon Preached in Lambeth Chapel at the Consecration of the Right Reverend Father in God Thomas Lord Bishop of Chichester on Sunday October 7, 1722* (London, 1722), pp. 1–23. The last quote is on p. 15. The Jewish expositor on the verse, to whom he referred, was either Rashi or Sforno. Both mention the *Shekhinah,* the divine presence, resting upon Aaron and the Levites.

28. Oxford Bodl. Ms. Eng. th.e. 140, f.327.

29. Oxford Bodl. Ms. Eng. th.e. 141, f.20, 181.

30. Oxford Bodl. Ms. Eng. th.e. 141, f.384.

31. Oxford Bodl. Ms. Eng. th.e. 142, f.335. Wilkins's citations of Jewish legal

sources might also be based on his intimate familiarity with the corpus of John Selden's writing, which he edited. Whatever the other sources of Wilkins's extensive rabbinic knowledge, Selden was surely a profound mentor to him in this regard. My thanks to Professor Jason Rosenblatt for underscoring this point for me.

32. Oxford Bodl. Ms. Eng. th.e. 142, f.406–9.

33. Oxford. Bodl. Ms. Eng. th.e. 143, f.73, 75, 76, 85, 103.

34. Oxford Bodl. Ms. Eng. th.e. 144, f.6

35. Oxford Bodl. Ms. Eng. th.e. 145, f.267–74.

36. Oxford Bodl. Ms. Eng. th.e. 146, f.119–20. See, for example, B.T. Shabbat 119a, 139a; Yoma 9b. A large list of rabbinic sources on the reasons for the Temple's destruction is found in Louis Ginzberg, *The Legends of the Jews* (Philadelphia, 1968), 6:388, n. 16.

37. Oxford Bodl. Ms. Eng. th.e. 147, f.124, 129. On Prideaux's view on the subject and the Jewish response of David Levi, see David B. Ruderman, *Jewish Enlightenment in an English Key* (Princeton, N.J., 2000), pp. 81, 177.

38. See, for example, Oxford Bodl. Ms. Eng. th.e. 141, f.413–15, 420–24; 143, f.293, 316–17, 330; 145, f.107, 111–12, 130–34, 233, 327; 147, f.251–84; 148, f.55, 63.

39. Here are some examples of his use of the acronym: Oxford Bodl. Eng. th.e.144, f.57; 145, f.1, 263, 335; 146, f.213, 519; British Library Ms. Add. 11628, f.1; British Library Ms. Add A. 182, f.131a, 138a.

40. British Library Ms. Sloane 4055, f.163.

41. *List of Additions to the Manuscripts in the British Museum in the Years MDCC-CXXXVI–MDCCCXL* (London, 1843), p. 13.

42. British Library Ms. Eg. 792 entitled "Jewish Liturgy translated by David Wilkins," f.96, 97, 99, 101, 108, 113, 118, 121, 127, 140, 143, 152–53, 155, 157, 160, 171, 178–79. On prayers for protection against demons, see Joshua Trachtenberg, *Jewish Magic and Superstition: A Study in Folk Religion* (New York, 1970), pp. 155–56. On the impact of Kabbalah and especially Lurianic kabbalah on the liturgy, his hymns, and his so-called *Siddur ha-Ari*, see generally A. Z. Idelsohn, *Jewish Liturgy and Its Development* (New York, 1932), pp. 47–55; Gershom Scholem, *On the Kabbalah and Its Symbolism* (New York, 1965), pp. 118–57; and more recently, Pinchas Giller, "Between Poland and Jerusalem: Kabbalistic Prayer in Early Modern Judaism," *Modern Judaism* 24 (2004): 226–50.

43. The reference is to the custom of *tikkun leil Hoshana Rabba*. See also Zedekiah ben Abraham Anav, *Sefer Shibbolei Leket ha-Shalem*, ed. Solomon Buber (Vilna, 1886), p. 34.

44. British Library Ms. Eg. 191, f.182, 196, 210, 217, 218.

45. Ibid., f.219–75.

46. On the first English translations of the Hebrew prayer book, see Ruderman, *Jewish Enlightenment in an English Key*, pp. 231–40; Simeon Singer, "Early Translation and Translators of the Jewish Liturgy in England," *The Jewish Historical Society of England Transactions: Sessions 1896–8* (Edinburgh and London, 1899): 36–71. This text should be compared specifically with the prayer book of Abraham Meers, alias Gamaliel Ben Pedahzur, an Ashkenazic Jewish convert to Christianity, who published his book in 1738 in London. On him, see Ruderman, *Jewish Enlightenment in an English Key*, pp. 242–44; and Cecil Roth, "Gamaliel Ben Pedahzur and His Prayer Book," *Jewish Historical Society of England Miscellanies* 2 (1935): 1–8. It also should be compared with the first German translation of the Jewish prayer book by the convert Anthonius Margaritha in 1530. See Maria

Diemling, "Antonius Margaritha on the 'Whole Jewish Faith': A Sixteenth-Century Convert from Judaism and His Depiction of the Jewish Religion," in Dean Phillip Bell and Stephen G. Burnett, eds., *Jews, Judaism and the Reformation in Sixteenth-Century Germany* (Leiden, 2006), pp. 322–28.

47. British Library Ms. Eg. 792, f.276–77.

48. Ibid., f.277–78.

49. Ibid., f.278–79. As Jason Rosenblatt pointed out to me in private correspondence, Wilkins might have been indebted to John Selden's extensive discussions of converts in several of his works. Even more relevant to this homily is the commentary of John Lightfoot on Matt. 23:15 in his *Horae Hebraicae et Talmudicae* (Cambridge and London, 1658, 1663, 1671, 1674). It is obvious that Wilkins drew freely from it. See Jason Rosenblatt, *Renaissance England's Chief Rabbi: John Selden* (Oxford and New York, 2006), pp. 132–33. My thanks to Professor Rosenblatt for allowing me to read his book in galleys prior to publication.

50. British Library Ms. Eg. 792, f.279.

Chapter 3

1. Hart, "The Family of Mordecai Hamburger," pp. 57, 63–76, supplies some additional information on these brothers and sisters and their children.

2. Simon, *Genealogical Tables of Jewish Families,* unpaginated handwritten table. But compare Hart, "The Family of Mordecai Hamburger," pp. 63–64, which claims that Judith married Hyam Moses, the brother of Moses Marcus, and had two children, Jacob and Esther.

3. On Bryom, see J. R. Watson, "Byrom, John (1692–1763)," *Oxford Dictionary of National Biography,* http://www.oxforddnb.com/view/article/4278.

4. Richard Parkinson, ed., *The Private Journal and Literary Remains of John Byrom* (Manchester, 1854), vol. 1, pt. 2, pp. 389, 443. In the light of his garbled reference to "Canticles," it is worth noting that Byrom was particularly interested in the Psalms, writing a poem on the Twenty-third Psalm called "A Divine Pastoral" that gained him considerable fame. The word "Selah," a frequently concluding word in the Psalms, is generally considered to indicate a pause or musical annotation. I am unaware of its meaning as a contraction of three words.

5. On Lyons, see Thompson Cooper, "Lyons, Israel, the Elder (d. 1770)," rev. Philip Carter, *Oxford Dictionary of National Biography,* http://www.oxforddbn.com/view/article/17289. On his son, see Lynn B. Glyn, "Israel Lyons: A Short but Starry Career; The Life of an Eighteenth-Century Jewish Botanist and Astronomer," *Royal Society Annual Review* 56 (2002): 275–305.

6. Parkinson, *The Private Journal,* vol. 1, pt. 2, pp. 525, 531–32, 538.

7. Betty Wood, "Perceval, John, First Earl of Egmont (1683–1748)," *Oxford Dictionary of National Biography,* http://www.oxforddnb.com/view/article/21911.

8. John Perceval Egmont, *Manuscripts of the Earl of Egmont (1730–47),* 3 vols. (London, 1920–23), vol. 2 [*Diary of the First Earl of Egmont (Viscount Percival) 1734–38*], p. 276. On the designation of Marcus as "a converted Jew," see my discussion in the next chapter.

9. On Sloane and his colorful career as a scientist, collector, administrator, and benefactor, see Arthur Macgregor, "Sloane, Hans, Baronet (1660–1753)," *Oxford Dictionary of National Biography,* http://www.oxforddnb.com/view/article/25730.

10. British Library Ms. Sloane 4055, f.162–63.

11. I have not yet been able to identify this person with certainty. Perhaps he was the duke of Montague mentioned by Martin Folkes as his friend. See David Boyd Haycock, "Folkes, Martin (1690–1754)," *Oxford Dictionary of National Biography,* http://www.oxforddnb.com/view/article/9795.

12. On Gibson, see Norman Sykes, *Edmund Gibson, Bishop of London* (Oxford, 1926); Stephen Taylor, "Gibson, Edmond (bap. 1669–d.1748)," *Oxford Dictionary of National Biography,* http://www.oxforddnb.com/view/article/10615.

13. On Hoadley, see Norman Sykes, "Benjamin Hoadley," in *The Social and Political Ideas of Some English Thinkers of the Augustan Age,* ed. F. J. C. Hearnshaw (London, 1928); Gordon Rupp, *Religion in England 1688–1791* (Oxford, 1986), pp. 88–102; B. W. Young, *Religion and Enlightenment in Eighteenth-Century England* (Oxford, 1998); Stephen Taylor, "Hoadley, Benjamin (1676–1761)," *Oxford Dictionary of National Biography,* http://www.oxforddnb.com/view/article/13375.

14. Francoise Deconinck-Brossard, "Chandler, Edward (1668?–1750)," *Oxford Dictionary of National Biography,* http://www.oxforddnb.com/view/article/5101; see also, Chapter 4 in this volume.

15. British Library Ms. Sloane 4055, f.162–63.

16. British Library Add. Ms. 4377, f.34–35.

17. British Library Ms. Percy e. 9, part 1, f.1–116. The date is on f.116. See also Katz, *The Jews in the History of England,* p. 213, n. 92, which mentions Oxford Bodl. Ms. Mason AA, 499, where the following notation appears opposite the title page: "Moses Marcus taught me Hebrew. J. Sarum."

18. See Ruderman, *Jewish Enlightenment in an English Key,* pp. 244–49.

19. Moses Marcus, *The Ceremonies of the Present Jews* (London, 1729), p. iv.

20. Ibid., pp. iv–v.

21. Ibid., pp.vi–vii.

22. Ibid., pp. vii–x.

23. Ibid., pp x–xi.

24. Compare Carlebach, *Divided Souls,* pp. 170–77. See now the important Hebrew dissertation of Yaakov Deutsch, "Judaism in Christian Eyes: 'Ethnographic' Descriptions of Judaism in the Writings of Christian Scholars in Western Europe from the Sixteenth Century to the Middle of the Eighteenth Century" (Hebrew University, 2004). Deutsch looks at some sixty books similar to that of Marcus, whom he also cites, many of them written by converts from Judaism describing the religion they had elected to abandon and presenting similarly conflicted attitudes toward its faith and praxis.

25. Marcus, *The Ceremonies of the Present Jews,* pp. 29–30.

26. On Waterland, see B. W. Young, "Waterland, Daniel (1683–1740)," *Oxford Dictionary of National Biography,* http://www.oxforddnb.com/view/article/28815; Robert T. Holtby, *Daniel Waterland 1683–1740: A Study in Eighteenth-Century Orthodoxy* (Carlisle, 1966); J. C. D. Clark, *English Society 1660–1832: Religion, Ideology, and Politics During the Ancien Regime,* 2nd ed. (Cambridge, 2000), index; Young, *Religion and Enlightenment in Eighteenth-Century England,* pp. 14, 35–36, 100–106; John Redwood, *Reason, Ridicule, and Religion: The Age of Enlightenment in England 1660–1750* (London, 1976), index; M. Louise Cornell, "Stand for Orthodoxy in the English Church: The Work of Daniel Waterland," *Didaskalia* 7 (1996): 56–62.

27. On Middleton, see John A. Duessinger, "Middleton, Conyers (1683–1750)," *Oxford Dictionary of National Biography,* http://www.oxforddnb.comn/view/article/18669; John Gascoigne, *Cambridge in the Age of Enlightenment: Science, Religion, and Politics from the Restoration to the French Revolution* (Cambridge, 1989), pp. 136–37;

T. Q. Campbell, "John Wesley, Conyers Middleton, and Divine Intervention in History," *Church History* 55 (1986): 39–59.

28. On Pearce, see Robert Hole, "Pearce, Zachary (1690–1774)," *Oxford Dictionary of National Biography,* http://oxforddnb.com/view/article/21693.

29. Daniel Waterland, *Scripture Vindicated in Answer to a Book Intituled* Christianity as Old as the Creation (London, 1730), pt. 1, pp. 56–64. The quote is on p. 56.

30. Conyers Middleton, *A Letter to Dr. Waterland: containing some Remarks on his Vindication of Scripture: in answer to a book, intituled,* Christianity as Old as the Creation. *Together with the sketch, or plan, of another answer to the said book* (London, 1931), pp. 25–38. On Spenser, see chapter 6, n. 37; on Lightfoot, see chapter 6, n. 16.

31. Zachary Pearce, *A Reply to the Letter to Dr. Waterland Setting Forth the many Falsehoods in the Quotations and the Historical Facts by which the Letter-writer endeavours to weaken the Authority of Moses* (London, 1731), pp. 29–31.

32. [Moses Marcus], *An Answer to the Letter to Dr. Waterland; in relation to the Point of Circumcision, wherein the Letter-writer's gross mistakes are examin'd and confuted* (London, 1731), pp. 3–5.

33. Ibid., pp. 9–31.

34. Ibid., p. 32.

35. Conyers Middleton, *A Defence of the Letter to Dr. Waterland against the False and Frivolous Cavils of the Author of the Reply* (London, 1732), pp. 18–19, 56–57.

36. Zachary Pearce, *A Reply to the Defence of the Letter to Dr. Waterland by the Author of the Reply to the Letter* (London, 1732), pp. 28–29, 31.

37. Waterland, *Scripture Vindicated,* p. 111.

38. Edward Churton, ed., *Fourteen Letters from Daniel Waterland to Zachary Pearce* (Oxford and London, 1868), p. 23.

Chapter 4

1. On Whiston, see Stephen D. Snobelen, "Whiston, William (1667–1752)," *Oxford Dictionary of National Biography,* http://www.oxforddnb.com/view/article/29217; James E. Force, *William Whiston, Honest Newtonian* (Cambridge, 1985); Maureen Farrell, *William Whiston* (New York, 1981); Stephen D. Snobelen, "William Whiston: Natural Philosopher, Prophet, Primitive Christian" (Ph.D. diss., Cambridge University, 2000).

2. William Whiston, *The Accomplishment of Scripture Prophecies Being Eight Sermons Preach'd at the Cathedral Church of St. Paul in the year MDCCVII at the Lecture founded by the Honourable Rober Boyle Esq.* (London, 1708), p. 13.

3. Ibid., p. 16.

4. Ibid., p. 17.

5. William Whiston, *A Supplement to the Literal Accomplishment of Scripture Prophecies containing Observations on Dr. Clarke's and Bishop Chandler's late Discourses of the Prophecies of the Old Testament* (London, 1725), pp. 5–6.

6. William Whiston, *An Essay Towards Restoring the True Text of the Old Testament and for Vindicating the Citations made thence in the New Testament to which is subjoined a large Appendix* (London, 1722), pp. 220 (proposition xii), and 281 (proposition xiii).

7. Whiston, *An Essay Towards Restoring the True Text,* pp. 223–24.

8. Ibid., p. 333. On the project of Kennicott and Lowth, see Ruderman, *Jewish Enlightenment in an English Key,* chaps. 1 and 2; and David Katz, *God's Last*

Words: Reading the English Bible from the Reformation to Fundamentalism (New Haven, 2004).

9. William Whiston, *A Supplement to Mr. Whiston's late Essay towards restoring the true Text of the Old Testament proving that the Canticles is not a Sacred Book of the Old Testament, nor was originally esteemed as such, either by the Jewish or the Christian Church* (London, 1723).

10. Johann Gottlob Carpzov, *Critica sacra veteris testamenti*, 3 vols. (Leipzig, 1723). Marcus translated 3:779–979. On Carpzov, see *Jewish Encyclopedia* (New York, 1901–6), 3:592; Rudolf Smend, "Spätorthodoxe Antikritik: Zum Werk des Johann Gottlob Carpzov," in Henning von Graf Reventlow et al., eds., *Historische kritik und biblischer kanon in der deutschen Aufklärung* (Wiesbaden, 1988), pp. 127–37. Carpzov's portrait is included in his edition of Thomas Goodwin's work, entitled *Apparatus Historico Criticus Antiquitatum sacri codicis et gentis Hebraeae uberimis annotationibus in Thomae Goodwini Mosen et Aaronem subministravit* (Leipzig, 1748).

11. Moses Marcus, ed. and trans., *A Defence of the Hebrew Bible in Answer to the Charge of Corruption Brought Against it by Mr. Whiston in his Essay towards restoring the true Text of the Old Testament, wherein Mr. Whiston's Pretences are particularly Examined and Confuted, by the Reverend Dr. Carpzov of Leipsick* (London, 1729), pp. iv–vii. On le Clerc, see below Chapter 6, n. 16; on Vossius and Simon, see Chapter 6, n. 14. On Stephanus Morinus (1624–1700) and his *Exercitationes de lingue primaeva* (Utrecht, 1694), see Noco Adriaan van Uchelen, "The Jewish Sources of Morinus's *Exercitationes*," *Dutch Jewish History* 3 (1993): 127–35. On Lewis Cappellus (1585–1658) and his *Commentarii et notae criticae in Vetus Testamentum* (Amsterdam, 1689), see George Hermann Schnedermann, *Die Controverse des L. Cappellus mit den Buxtorfen über das Alter des hebräische Punctation: Ein Beitrag zuder Geschichte des Studiums der hebräischen Sprache* (Leipzig, 1879). On Paul Pezron (1639–1706), see his *L'Antiquité des Tems rétablie et défendué contre les Juifs et les nouveaux chronologis* (Paris, 1687), and his *Défense de l'Antiquité des Tems, où l'on soûtient la tradition des Pères et des Églises, contra celle du Talmud; et où l'on fait voir la corruption de l'Hébreu des Juifs* (Paris, 1691).

12. Marcus, *A Defence of the Hebrew Bible*, pp. ix–x.

13. On the Isaacs, see Carlebach, *Divided Souls*, pp. 36, 60–62, 123, 128–29, 163–64; idem, "Jewish Responses to Christianity in Reformation Germany," in Dean Phillip Bell and Stephen G. Burnett, eds. *Jews, Judaism, and the Reformation in Sixteenth-Century Germany* (Leiden, 2006), pp. 467–69; William Rotscheidt, *Stephan Isaak: Ein Kölner Pfarrer und Hessischer Superintendent im Reformationsjahrhundert* (Leipzig, 1910); Hava Fraenkel-Goldschmidt, "On the Periphery of Jewish Society: Jewish Converts to Christianity in the Age of the Reformation (Hebrew)," in *Tarbut ve-Ḥevrah be-Toledot Yisra'el bimai ha-Beinayim [Festschrift in honor of . . . Ḥayyim Hillel Ben Sasson]* (Jerusalem, 1989), pp. 623–54; and *Jewish Encyclopedia* (New York, 1901–6), 6:623. Johannes's book is entitled *Defensio Veritatis Hebraicae Sacrarum Scripturarum, adversus . . . vilhelmi Lindani S.T. Doctoris, quos de optimo Scripturas interpretandi genere inscripsit* (Cologne, 1559). The reference to this work in Carpzov's text is in Marcus, *A Defence of the Hebrew Bible*, p. 145.

14. I am indebted to a conversation with Andrea Schatz for this emphasis. Compare also the illuminating comments in Amnon Raz-Krakotskin, "Censorship, Editing, and the Reshaping of Jewish Identity: The Catholic Church and Hebrew Literature in the Sixteenth Century," in Allison P. Coudert and Jeffrey S. Shoulson, eds., *Hebraica Veritas? Christian Hebraists and the Study of Judaism in Early Modern Europe,* (Philadelphia, 2004), p. 136: "The converts' functions in the print

shops were based on similar criteria to those employed by Jews and Christian Hebraists, even after their conversion. They saw themselves as bearers of the Hebrew tradition and aspired to preserve it. Converts who were employed as editors emphasized their Jewish origins in the colophons added to the printed books. . . . The work of the converts in the printing process, both as editors and censors, reflects a dialogue between the two sides of their identity." The converts working in the Hebrew printing business and Moses Marcus shared a common objective of preserving faithfully the texts they had studied as Jews, which now assumed a vital part of their new identity as "converted Jews."

15. Marcus, *A Defence of the Hebrew Bible,* pp. xii–xiii.

16. On Levi, see Ruderman, *Jewish Enlightenment in an English Key.*

17. Carpzov refers, of course, to the *Theological Political Treatise* of Benedict Spinoza (1632–77). On this, see, for example, Leo Strauss, *Spinoza's Critique of Religion* (New York, 1965). On Grotius's biblical studies, see, for example, Jean-Paul Heering, *Hugo Grotius as Apologist for the Christian Religion: A Study of His Work* De veritate religionis Christianae, 1640 (Leiden, 2004); A. W. Rosenberg, "Hugo Grotius as Hebraist," *Studia Rosenthaliana* 12 (1978): 62–90; and François Leplanche, "Le canon de l'Ancient Testament dans la controverse entre catholiques et protestants au XVIIe siècle, le point de Grotius," in Michel Tardieu, ed., *La formation des canons scripturaires,* (Paris, 1993), pp. 107–22. On le Clerc, see Martin I. Klauber, "Between Protestant Orthodoxy and Rationalism: Fundamental Articles in the Early Career of Jean LeClerc," *Journal of the History of Ideas* 54 (1993): 611–36; M. C. Pitassi, *Entre croire et savoir: Le probleme de la methode critique chez Jean Le Clerc* (Leiden, 1987); and Samuel Golden, *Jean LeClerc* (New York, 1972). On Cappellus, see above, n. 11.

18. Marcus, *A Defence of the Hebrew Bible,* author's preface, pp. ii–iv; 4, 7, 13–15, 37 [note of Marcus], 45, 52, 53, 57, 82, 92.

19. Ibid., pp. 104, 113, 123.

20. Ibid., pp. 310, 329, 330, 331.

Chapter 5

1. On Collins, see J. Dybikowski, "Collins, Anthony (1676–1729)," *Oxford Dictionary of National Biography,* http://www.oxforddnb.com/view/article/5933. See also Rupp, *Religion in England* pp. 265–72, and see the additional works on him below.

2. Anthony Collins, *A Discourse of the Grounds and Reasons of the Christian Religion in two parts . . . The second containing an Examination of the Scheme advanc'd by Mr. Whiston in his Essay towards restoring the true text of the Old Testament, and for vindicating the Citations thence made in the New Testament* (London, 1724), p. xliii.

3. Ibid., p. 111.

4. Ibid., p. 225.

5. Ibid., p. 112.

6. Ibid., pp. 53–58.

7. Ibid., pp. 61, 62–78, 92, 93, 95, 269.

8. William Whiston, *The Literal Accomplishment of Scripture Prophecies being a full Answer to a late Discourse, of the Grounds and Reasons of the Christian Religion* (London, 1724), pp. 7, 16.

9. Whiston, *A Supplement to the Literal Accomplishment of Scripture,* pp. 35, 39, 40.

10. On Isaac of Troki, see Róbert Dán, "Isaac Troky and His 'Antitrinitarian' Sources," in Róbert Dán, ed., *Occident and Orient: A Tribute to the Memory of Alexander Scheiber* (Budapest, 1988), pp. 69–82; Stefan Schreiner, "Rabbinitische Quellen im 'Buch der Stärkung des Glaubens' des Karäers Isaak ben Abraham aus Troki," *Frankfurter Judaistische Beiträge* 26 (1999): 51–92, as well as his other studies on him. A new book by the late Richard Popkin on Troki is slated to appear in the near future. On Saul Levi Morteira, see the many essays by Marc Saperstein, including "Christianity, Christians, and 'New Christians' in the Sermons of Saul Levi Morteira," *Hebrew Union College Annual* 70–71 (1999–2000): 329–84, and most recently, *Exile in Amsterdam: Saul Levi Morteira's Sermons to a Congregation of "New Jews"* (Cincinnati, 2005). On Isaac Orobrio de Castro, see Yosef Kaplan, *From Christianity to Judaism: The Story of Isaac Orobrio de Castro* (London, 1989).

11. James O'Higgens, S.J., *Anthony Collins: The Man and His Works* (The Hague, 1970), pp. 31–32, 38, 167–68, 170–73.

12. David Berman, *A History of Atheism in Britain from Hobbes to Russell* (London and New York, 1990), pp. 70–87; and idem, "Deism, Immorality, and the Art of Lying," in J. A. Leo Lemay, ed., *Deism, Masonry, and the Enlightenment, Essays Honoring Alfred Owen Aldridge* (Newark, Dela., 1987), pp. 61–78, especially 66.

13. Pascal Taranto, *Du deisme à l'atheisme: La libre-pensée d'Anthony Collins* (Paris, 2000), especially pp. 13–20, 80–86.

14. Henning Graf Reventlow, *The Authority of the Bible and the Rise of the Modern World* (London, 1984), pp. 354–68.

15. Stephen Snobelen, "The Argument over Prophecy: An Eighteenth-Century Debate between William Whiston and Anthony Collins," *Lumen* 15 (1996): 195–213.

16. Hans W. Frei, *The Eclipse of Biblical Narrative: A Study in Eighteenth- and Nineteenth-Century Hermeneutics* (New Haven and London, 1974), pp. 66–85.

17. Thomas Sherlock, *The Use and Intent of Prophecy in the Several Ages of the World in Six Discourses delivered at the Temple Church in April and May, 1724* (London, 1725), pp. 33–35, 43, 48, 77–78. On Sherlock, see Colin Haydon, "Sherlock, Thomas (1677–1761)," *Oxford Dictionary of National Biography*, http://www.oxforddnb.com/view/article/25380.

18. Edward Chandler, *A Defence of Christianity from the Prophecies of the Old Testament wherein are considered all the Objections against this Kind of Proof Advanced in a Late Discourse of the Grounds and Reasons of the Christian Religion,* 2nd ed. (London, 1725), especially pp. i–iv, 49, 58, 124, 117, 213, 221–23, 255–57, 260, 264, 266. He cites Surenhusius on pp. 222, 233, and 310.

19. On Michel de la Roche, see R. Julian Roberts, "Roche, Michael de la (c. 1680–1742)," *Oxford Dictionary of National Biography*, http://www.oxforddnb.com/view/article/23913; Uta Janssens-Knorsch, "Michel de la Roche," in Wiep van Bunge et al., eds., *Dictionary of Seventeenth- and Eighteenth-Century Dutch Philosophers* (Bristol, 2003), 2:845–47; Walter Graham, *English Literary Periodicals* (New York, 1930), pp. 196–99; Margaret D. Thomas, "Michel de la Roche," in Jean Sgard, ed., *Dictionnaire des journalistes* (Oxford, 1999); idem, "Michel de la Roche: A Huguenot Critic of Calvin," *Studies on Voltaire and the Eighteenth Century* 238 (1985): 97–195; George King, "Michel de la Roche et ses Mémoires Litteraires de la Grande Bretagne," *Revue de literature comparée* 15 (1943): 298–300. For the larger context of the community to which de la Roche belonged, see Ann Goldgar, *Impolite Learning: Conduct and Community in the Republic of Letters 1680–1750* (New Haven, Conn., 1995); and Joseph Almagor, *Pierre Desmaizeaux (1673–1745): Journalist and English Correspondent for Franco-Dutch Periodicals, 1700–20* (Amsterdam,

1989). Desmaizeaux, like de la Roche, was a Huguenot refugee, with an even more prominent profile in radical circles of London, being an especially close associate of Anthony Collins.

20. See de la Roche, *Memoirs of Literature* 3 (London, 1722), pp. 351–59; 7 (London, 1722), pp. 82–87, 393–97; 2 (London, 1722), p. 317; 4 (London, 1722), pp. 11–14, 314–19; idem, *New Memoirs of Literature* 3 (London, 1726), pp. 102–7; 5 (London, 1727), pp. 14–16.

21. De la Roche, *New Memoirs of Literature* 1 (London, 1725), pp. 348–49.

22. De la Roche, *New Memoirs of Literature* 2 (London, 1725), pp. 81–103. The citation is on p. 92. On Sykes, see John Stephens, "Sykes, Arthur Ashley (c. 1684–1756)," *Oxford Dictionary of National Biography,* http://www.oxforddnb.com/view/article/26867.

23. De la Roche, *New Memoirs of Literature* 2:92, 99, 103.

24. De la Roche, *Memoirs of Literature* 1 (London, 1722), pp. 116–120. The citations are on p. 117.

25. De la Roche, *Memoirs of Literature* 6 (London, 1722), pp. 110–18. The citations are on pp. 110–11. Surenhusius's book is entitled: *[Sefer ha-Mashveh] sive in quo secundum veterum Theologorum Hebraeorum Formulas allegandi, & Mosos Intepretandi Conciliantur loca ex. V. in N.T. allegata Auctore Guililelmo Surenhusio, Hebraicarum & Graecarum Literarum in Illustri Amsteliaedamensium Athenaeo Professore* (Amsterdam, 1713).

26. De la Roche, *Memoirs of Literature* 6:113.

27. Ibid., 115, 117.

28. Ibid., 117.

29. Ibid., 131. This entire installment runs on pp. 131–54. Additional material on Nicholas Antoine was published by Julien Weill, "Nicolas Antoine: Un Pasteur protestant brulé a Genève en 1632 pour crime de Judaisme," *Revue des études juives* 36 (1898): 161–98; 37 (1898): 161–80. Compare the other cases of conversions to Judaism collected in the volume of Mulsow and Popkin, *Secret Conversions to Judaism in Early Modern Europe,* especially the article of Martin Mulsow himself.

30. See Thomas, "Michel de la Roche: A Huguenot Critic of Calvin," especially pp. 160–62.

31. Thomas, "Michel de la Roche," pp. 162–63, cited from de la Roche, *Memoirs of Literature* 1:60. On Clagett, see Warren Johnston, "Clagett, Nicholas (bap. 1654, d. 1727)," *Oxford Dictionary of National Biography,* http://www/oxforddnb.com/view/article/5424.

32. Compare Thomas, "Michel de la Roche," p. 163, which questions the sincerity of de la Roche's praise of Surenhusius, viewing the Anthoine story "as a counter to Surenhusius' work." I am not sure what she means by "a counter" in this context. I am convinced she is wrong about Michel de la Roche's sincerity in appreciating Surenhusius's book.

33. De la Roche, *Memoirs of Literature* 6:150, 152, 154.

34. Ibid., 184–92. Citations are from pp. 184 and 188.

35. The auction catalogue of his private library is extant and was published in Amsterdam in 1730 as *Bibliotheca Surenhusiana.* Even a casual look at its contents suggests the remarkably high level of Surenhusius's Hebraic knowledge. What is especially impressive are the titles of sixteenth- and seventeenth-century books in all fields, from halakha to Kabbalah, science, history, moral literature and more. Some examples include works of Samuel Zarza, Shem Tov ibn Shem Tov, Moses Isserles, Azariah Figo, Moses Cordovero, Isaac Gikatilia, Judah Moscato, Joseph

Karo, Isaac Taitaẓak, David del Bene, Menasseh ben Israel, Isaac Aboab, Yair Bachrach, Menahem Azariah de Fano, Joseph Delmedigo, Tobias Cohen, David Gans, David Nieto, and more.

36. Giulielmus Surenhusius, *Mischna sive Totius Hebraeorum Juris, Rituum, Antiquitatuum, ac Legum Oralium Systema, cum clarissimorum Rabbinorum Maimonides & Barrnotae Commentariis Integris,* 6 vols. (Amsterdam, 1698–1703), especially vol. 1, *Praefatio ad Lectorem.* On Surenhusius and his work on the Mishnah, see the Dutch article by Peter van Rooden, "Willem Surenhis' Opuatting van de Misjna," in Jan de Roos, Arie Schippers, and Jan W. Wesselius, eds., *Driehonderd jaar oosterse talen in Amsterdam* (Amsterdam, 1986), pp. 43–54; the almost identical English article by the same author, "The Amsterdam Translation of the Mishnah," in William Horbury, ed., *Hebrew Study from Ezra to Ben-Yehuda* (Edinburgh, 1999), pp. 257–67; Jan W. Wesselius, "De briefwisseling tussen Johann Christoffer Wolf en Willem Surenhuisen (1720–27)," *Studia Rosenthaliana* 26 (1992): 136–48; Annelies Kuyt and Emile Schrijver, "Translating the Mishnah in the Northern Netherlands: A Tentative Bibliographie Raisonnée," in Annelies Kuyt and N. A. van Uchelen, eds., *History and Form: Dutch Studies in the Mishnah* (Amsterdam, 1988), pp. 1–42, especially 15–25.

Chapter 6

1. On William Wotton, see David Stoker, "William Wotton (1666–1727)," *Oxford Dictionary of National Biography,* http://www.oxforddnb.com/view/article/30005; Joseph M. Levine, *The Battle of the Books: History and Literature in the Augustine Age* (Ithaca, N.Y. and London, 1991); A. R. Hall, "William Wotton and the History of Science," *Archives Internationales d'Histoire des Sciences* 9 (1949): 1047–62.

2. On Ockley, see Peter M. Holt, "Ockley, Simon (bap. 1679, d. 1720)," *Oxford Dictionary of National Biography,* http://www.oxforddnb.com/view/article/20494; Azza Kararah, "Simon Ockley: His Contribution to Arabic Studies and Influence on Western Thought" (Ph.D. diss., Cambridge University, 1955); Arthur J. Arberry, *Oriental Essays: Portraits of Seven Scholars* (Richmond, Surrey, 1977), pp. 11–47; Holt, "The Treatment of Arabic History by Prideaux, Ockley, and Sale," pp. 290–302, reprinted in Peter M. Holt, *Studies in the History of the Near East* (London, 1973), pp. 50–63.

3. British Library Add. Ms. 23204, f.6a-6b. On Abendana, see David S. Katz, "The Abendana Brothers and the Christian Hebraists of Seventeenth-Century England," *Journal of Ecclesiastical History* 40 (1989): 28–52; Jan Wilhelm Wesselius, "I Don't Know Whether He Will Stay for Long: Isaac Abendana's Early Years in England and His Latin Translation of the Mishnah," *Studia Rosenthaliana* 22 (1988): 85–96; Israel Abrahams, "Isaac Abendana's Cambridge Mishnah and Oxford Calendars," *Transactions of the Jewish Historical Society of England* 8 (1915–17), 98–121. See also Ernestine van der Wall, "The Dutch Hebraist Adam Boreel and the Mishnah Project," *Lias* 16 (1989): 239–63; Richard Popkin, "Some Aspects of Jewish-Christian Theological Interchanges in Holland and England 1640–1700," in Jan van den Berg and Ernestine van der Wall, eds., *Jewish-Christian Relations in the Seventeenth Century: Studies and Documents* (Dordrecht, 1988), pp. 8–11; and Richard Popkin, "Two Treasures of Marsh's Library," in Allison Coudert, Sarah Hutton, Richard Popkin, and Gordon Weiner, eds., *Judaeo-Christian Intellectual Culture in the Seventeenth Century* (Dordrecht, 1999), pp. 1–12. On Constantijn

L'Empereur and his *Clavis Talmudica,* see Peter T. Van Rooden, *Theology, Biblical Scholarship and Rabbinical Studies in the Seventeenth Century: Constanijn L'Empereur (1591–1648), Professor of Hebrew and Theology at Leiden* (Leiden, 1989). On the earlier attempts to translate the Mishnah, including that of William Guise, see Mordechai Feingold, "Oriental Studies," in Nicholas Tyacke, ed., 1997 *Seventeenth-Century Oxford* (Oxford, 1997), pp. 449–503, especially 465; Gerald J. Toomer, *Eastern Wisedome and Learning: The Study of Arabic in Seventeenth-Century England* (Oxford, 1996), p. 293; and Alastair Hamilton, "Guise, William (Bap. 1652–d. 1683)," *Oxford Dictionary of National Biography,* http://www.oxforddnb.com/view/article/1729. Guise's Latin translation of the tractate of *Zera'im* was published posthumously by his colleague Edward Bernard in 1690.

4. Simon Ockley, *The History of the Present Jews Throughout the World being an Ample tho Succinct Account of their Ceremonies, and Manner of Living, at this time, trans. From the Italian, written by Leo Modena a Venetian Rabbi . . . Two Supplements . . . The Samaritans . . . Carraites, from the French of Father Simon* (London, 1707), preface. On Leon Modena, see Mark R. Cohen, ed., *The Autobiography of a Seventeenth-Century Venetian Rabbi* (Princeton, N.J., 1988); and his "Leone da Modena's *Riti*: A Seventeenth-Century Plea for Social Toleration of Jews," *Jewish Social Studies* 34 (1972): 287–319, republished in David Ruderman, ed., *Essential Papers on Jewish Culture in Renaissance and Baroque Italy* (New York, 1992), pp. 429–73.

5. Cambridge Ms. 7113, letter 33, Wotton to Ockley. My sincere thanks go to my student Andrew Berns, who kindly read through this manuscript containing twenty-one letters to Simon Ockley, summarized them for me, and also sent me copies of the originals.

6. British Library Ms. Harley 6941, f.230b-231a.

7. Cambridge Ms. 7113, letter 34, Wotton to Ockley.

8. British Library Add. Ms. 5831, Wotton to Dr. Walker, f.124a.

9. Ibid., f.125a.

10. Cambridge Ms. 7113, letter 45, Wotton to Ockley.

11. Ibid., letter 39, May 9, 1717, and letter 40, May 31, 1717, Wotton to Ockley.

12. Ibid., letter 46, Wotton to Ockley.

13. William Wotton, *Miscellaneous Discourses Relating to the Traditions and Uses of the Scribes and Pharisees in the Blessed Saviour Jesus Christ's Time,* 2 vols. (London, 1718), pp. i–iv.

14. Ibid., pp. v–xxvi. On Vossius, see Thomas Seccombe, "Vossius, Isaac (1618–1689)," rev. F. F. Blok, *Oxford Dictionary of National Biography,* http://www.oxforddnb.com/view/article/28356; David S. Katz, "Isaac Vossius and the English Biblical Critics 1670–1689," in Richard Popkin and Arjo Vanderjagt, eds., *Scepticism and Irreligion in the Seventeenth and Eighteenth Centuries* (Leiden, 1993), pp. 142–84; F. F. Blok, *Isaac Vossius and His Circle: His Life until His Farewell to Queen Christina of Sweden 1618–1655* (Groningen, 2000). Wotton referred to Vossius's well-publicized work on biblical chronology, preferring the dating of the Septuagint over that of the original Hebrew version of the Bible, and his advocacy of the reliability of the Sibylline Oracles in predicting the coming of Christ. He was refuted by Richard Simon (1638–1712) in his *Critical Enquiries into the Various Editions of the Bible Printed in divers Places and at several times: together with Animadversions upon a small Treatise of Dr. Isaac Vossius concerning the Oracles of the Sibylls, and an Answer to the Objections of the late Critica sacra* (London, 1684), published first in Latin a short time earlier. On Richard Simon, the literature is vast. See, for example, Miriam Yardeni, "La vision des Juifs et du Judaism dan L'oeuvre de Richard

Simon," *Revue des études juives* 128 (1970): 179–203; Jean Steinmann, *Richard Simon et les origins d'éxegese biblique* (Paris, 1960); Justin Champion, "Pere Richard Simon and English Biblical Criticism 1680–1700," in James E. Force and David S. Katz, eds., *Everything Connects: In Conference with Richard H. Popkin; Essays in His Honor* (Leiden, 1999), pp. 39–61. On earlier Latin translations of the Mishnah, see Feingold, "Oriental Studies," and the other sources mentioned above in n. 3, especially to L'Empereur. On Cocceius, see Willem J. van Asselt, *The Federal Theology of Johannes Cocceius (1603–1669)* (Leiden, 2001); Adina Yoffie, "Cocceius and the Jewish Commentators," *Journal of the History of Ideas* 65 (2004): 383–98. On Sheringham and his *Joma Codex Talmudicus* (London, 1648), see Alastair Hamilton, "Sheringham, Robert (c. 1604–78)," *Oxford Dictionary of National Biography,* http://www.oxforddnb.com/view/article/25375. *The Praefatio ad lectorum* of his translation offers a strong case for the use of rabbinic materials, including the Talmud, in contextualizing the New Testament.

15. Wotton, *Miscellaneous Discourses,* p. xlvii.

16. Ibid., p. xlix. On Scaliger (1540–1609), see Anthony Grafton, *Joseph Scaliger: A Study in the History of Classical Scholarship,* 2 vols. (Oxford, 1983–93). Pococke's fame mainly rested on his Arabic scholarship, but his *Porta Mosis* (Oxford, 1655), on Maimonides's commentary on the Mishnah, was an important contribution to the field. Pococke also influenced an entire generation of rabbinic scholars such as Guise, Sheringham, and Samuel Clarke (1624–69). His work is nicely summarized by Gerald J. Toomer, "Pococke, Edward (1604–91)," *Oxford Dictionary of National Biography,* http://www.oxforddnb.com/view.article/22430. John Lightfoot (1602–74) was clearly one of the chief pioneers in using rabbinic sources to elucidate the text and context of the New Testament, especially in his *Horae Hebraicae et Talmudicae.* See Newton E. Key, "Lightfoot, John (1602–1675)," *Oxford Dictionary of National Biography,* http://www.oxforddnb.com/view/article/16648; Frank Manuel, *The Broken Staff: Judaism through Christian Eyes* (Cambridge, Mass., 1992), pp. 130–32. John Selden (1584–1654) made his primary contribution in the use of rabbinic sources in his massive studies of the Noachide laws, marriage law, the Sanhedrin, the laws of tithes, and more. Some of the recent work on him is listed in Paul Christianson, "Selden, John (1584–1654)," *Oxford Dictionary of National Biography,* http://www.oxforddnb.com/view/article/25052. See especially the important new book of Jason Rosenblatt, *Renaissance England's Chief Rabbi.* Wotton explicitly mentions his reading Selden's work in a letter he wrote to William Bowyer in 1726. See Rosenblatt, *Renaissance England's Chief Rabbi,* p. 159, n. 6.

17. I have reproduced the entire chapter, with annotations, in Appendix 2 below.

18. See especially Rosenblatt, *Renaissance England's Chief Rabbi,* especially chaps. 6 and 7, pp. 135–57, 158–81, and the conclusion, 259–78.

19. See Lightfoot, *Horae Hebraicae et Talmudicae,* introduction to the commentary on Matthew. I have conveniently used the English translation offered by Philologos Religious Online Books, entitled John Lightfoot, *A Commentary on the New Testament from the Talmud and Hebraica,* http:/philologos.org_eb-jl/mattintr.htm.

20. Wotton, *Miscellaneous Discourses,* postscript of Mr. Simon Ockley, professor of Arabic at Cambridge, at the end of the preface.

21. Holt, "Ockley, Simon (bap. 1679, d. 1720)," in *Oxford Dictionary of National Biography,* mentions Ockley's obligation to Whiston to translate a part of the Arabic version of the *Didascalia,* the major part of the Apostolic Constitutions, a

text Whiston had relied on in reconstructing ancient Christianity. Realizing the controversy around Whiston, Ockley later attempted to distance himself from him.

22. Wotton, *Miscellaneous Discourses,* pp. 5–7, and see Appendix 2 below.

23. Ibid., pp. 38–40, 54–58, 71. On the Prosbul of Hillel, see *Encyclopedia Judaica* (Jerusalem, 1971) 13:1181–82.

24. Wotton, *Miscellaneous Discourses,* p. 78.

25. Ibid., p. 82.

26. Ibid., p. 118.

27. Ibid., pp. 96–101.

28. Ibid., pp. 121–70, 171–95, 196–203, 294–317.

29. British Library Add. Ms. 23204, f.37a.

30. Jeremy Collier, *A Vindication of the Reasons and Defence . . . Part 1, Being a Reply to the First Part of No Sufficient Reason for Restoring some Prayers and Directions of King Edward VI's First Liturgy* (London, 1718), pp. 39–45. On Collier, see Eric Salmon, "Collier, Jeremy (1650–1726)," *Oxford Dictionary of National Biography,* http://www.oxforddnb.com/view/article/5917.

31. William Wotton, *Some Thoughts Concerning a Proper Method of Studying Divinity* (London, 1734; Dublin and London, 1751), pp. 385–86.

32. Ibid., p. 398.

33. On Grotius and le Clerc, see Chapter 4, n. 17. On Pococke and Lightfoot, see above, n. 16. On Peter Allix (1641–1717), see Vivienne Larminie, "Allix Peter (1641–1717)," *Oxford Dictionary of National Biography,* http://www.oxforddnb. com/view/article/407, and especially Matt Goldish, "The Battle for 'True' Jewish Christianity: Peter Allix's Polemics against the Unitarians and Millenarians," in James E. Force and David S. Katz, eds., *Everything Connects: In Conference with Richard H. Popkin; Essays in His Honor* (Leiden, 1999), pp. 145–62. As Goldish points out, Allix, a Huguenot exile in London, is another interesting scholar and cleric with a wide and deep knowledge of rabbinic sources, who uses his erudition to attack Unitarians and millenarians alike. His position on the oral law also differentiates him from the other contemporary Christian scholars we have considered. Allix argued that indeed there was an oral law, that it was divine, and that it was crucial in understanding the written law. This oral law, if understood correctly, however, was not the one claimed by the rabbis but instead was one Allix had reconstructed to confirm the Trinity and Christian doctrine. This authentic version was later distorted by the rabbis who constructed their own false replica of the oral law. Only the kabbalists among medieval and contemporary Jews have preserved an authentic sense of the original and pure oral law as understood by Allix. Allix's argument, offered as a counterargument against the Unitarians who had claimed that their version of Christianity was closer to the authentic biblical faith, revealed his dexterity in using a Jewish argument about the need for an oral law to accompany the written in the service of Anglican orthodoxy. Goldish also discovered that Allix was the driving force behind the conversion of a North African Jewish merchant named Jonah Xeres. Xeres, probably with the direction and support of Allix himself, published *An Address to the Jews, by John Xeres: Containing His Reasons for Leaving the Jewish, and Embracing the Christian Religion* (London, 1710), a work reminiscent of the book Moses Marcus published fourteen years later. See Matt Goldish, "A Convert among the London Conversos: New Light on the Oral Law Debate," paper presented at the annual conference of the Association for Jewish Studies, December 2003. My thanks go to Professor Goldish for sharing this paper with me. On "Orobio the Jew," see Kaplan, *From Christianity to Judaism.*

34. Wotton, *Some Thoughts Concerning a Proper Method,* pp. 386, 398. His reference is to Claude Fleury (1640–1723) and his *Les moeurs des Israelites: Où l'on voit le modele d'une politique simple et sincere pour le gouvernement des états e la reforme des moeurs,* first published in Brussels in 1682 and subsequently in numerous editions in French and English. On Fleury, see Raymond Wanner, *Claude Fleury (1640–1723) as an Educational Historiographer and Thinker* (The Hague, 1975). On Buxtorf and his work, see Stephen Burnett, *From Christian Hebraism to Jewish Studies: Johannes Buxtorf (1564–1629) and Hebrew Learning in the Seventeenth Century* (Leiden, 1996).

35. Wotton, *Some Thoughts Concerning a Proper Method,* pp. 399–400.

36. Ibid., p. 400.

37. William Wotton, *Reflections upon Ancient and Modern Learning to which is now added a Defense thereof* (London, 1705), pp. 366–67. He refers to James Usher (1581–1656) and his *Annales Veteris Testamenti* (London, 1650); to John Marsham (1602–85) and his *Chronicus Canon Aegypticus, Ebraicus, Graecus* (London, 1666); to John Spencer (1630–93) and his *De legibus Hebraeorum ritualibus et earum rationibus* (London, 1727, and many earlier editions); and to Samuel Bochart (1599–1667) and his *Geographia sacra seu Phalag et Canaan* (London, 1707 and earlier editions).

38. Wotton, *Reflections on Ancient and Modern Learning,* p. 367.

Conclusion

1. See, for example, Frank Manuel, *The Broken Staff: Judaism through Christian Eyes* (Cambridge, Mass., 1992); Allison Coudert and Jeffrey Shoulson, eds., *Hebraica Veritas? Christian Hebraists, Jews, and the Study of Judaism in Early Modern Europe* (Philadelphia, 2004); Chaim Wirszubski, *Pico della Mirandola's Encounter with Jewish Mysticism* (Cambridge, Mass., 1989); Frances Yates, *The Occult Philosophy in the Renaissance* (London, 1979); Bernard McGinn, "Cabalists and Christians: Reflections on Cabala in Medieval and Renaissance Thought," in Richard Popkin and Gordon Weiner, eds., *Jewish Christians and Christian Jews: From the Renaissance to the Enlightenment* (Dordrecht, 1994), pp. 11–34; Jerome Friedman, *The Most Ancient Testimony: Sixteenth-Century Christian Hebraica in the Age of Renaissance Nostalgia* (Athens, Ohio, 1983); Burnett, *From Christian Hebraism to Jewish Studies*; and Deutsch, "Judaism in Christian Eyes." On the Christian scholars of the seventeenth century, especially in England, see my discussion in Chapter 5 above, and see Appendix 2 below.

2. Sutcliffe, *Judaism and Enlightenment,* and see my review of this book in the *Jewish Quarterly Review* 94 (2004): 523–30.

3. See especially the works of Justin Champion listed in the Introduction, n. 11.

Appendix 1

1. Jacob Campo Weyerman, ed., *De voornaamste beweegredenen en omstandigheden die aanleyding hebben geveeven aan Moses Marcus tot het verlaaten van dem Joodschen, en tot het aaneemen van den kristeyke Godsdienst* (Amsterdam, n.d.).

2. On Weyerman, see A. J. Hanou, "Jacob Campo Weyerman (1677–1747)," in Wiep van Bunge et al., eds., *Dictionary of Seventeenth and Eighteenth-Century*

Dutch Philosophers (Bristol, 2003), 2:1073–74; idem, "The Enlightened Authorship of Jacob Campo Weyerman (1677–1747)," *Dutch Crossing* 15 (1981): 3–22; Adele Nieuweboer, "Britain and the British in the Magazines of Jacob Campo Weyerman (1720–1730)," in *The Role of Periodicals in the Eighteenth Century* (Leiden, 1984), pp. 18–26; Margaret Jacob, *The Radical Enlightenment: Pantheists, Freemasons, and Republicans* (London, 1981), pp. 195–96; P. J. Buijnsters, *Nederlanse literatuur van de achttiende eeuw veertien ver kenningen* (Utrecht, 1984); W. P. Sautijn Kluit, "Jacob Campo Weyerman als journalist," *Nijhoff's Bijdragen tot de vanderlandsche geschiedeness*, nieuwe reeks, 7 (1872): 193–245; S. I. Eeghen, "Jacob Campo Weyerman en de boekhandel," *Mededelingen van de Stichting Jacob Campo Weyerman* 6 (1983): 1–16; P. Altena and W. Hendrikx, eds., *Het verlokkend oost: Proeven over Jacob Campo Weyerman* (Amsterdam, 1985). For additional bibliography, see the website of the Stichting Jacob Campo Weyerman, http://www.weyerman.nl and that of htttp://www.dnbl.org/auteurs. My thanks go to Professor Robert Naborn for the last references.

3. P. J. Buijnsters, "Jacob Campo Weyerman's 'Traktaat Tegen Het Jodendom," *Tijdschrift voor Nederlandse tall en letterkunde* 96 (1980): 38–56, from which almost all of my information is taken. See also H. Bovenkerk, "Nederlandse schrijvers tijdens de Republiek over de Joden," in H. Brugmans and A. Frank, eds., *Geschiedenis der Joden in Nederland,* vol. 1 (Amsterdam, 1940), pp. 741–43. I want to offer my thanks to Dr. A. K. Offenberg, a former librarian of the Bibliotheca Rosenthaliana, for introducing me to the Dutch version of Marcus's book and providing me with valuable information about Weyerman and William Surenhusius. I am also grateful to Dr. Piet Van Boxel of Oxford University for spending many hours with me, reading and translating the Dutch essays on Weyerman and Surenhusius.

Appendix 2

1. This is the way Wotton designates rabbinic legal literature. By the elders, he means the sages, the rabbis.

2. Note how Wotton understands the literary revival of his generation as being only 150 years old, spurred by the printing of classical works, especially Greek authors translated into Latin. This revival, he sadly points out, has not included the printing of the originals or the translations of rabbinic books. This underscores the innovative nature of his project and his need to "invent a tradition" of Christian scholarship on rabbinic literature that preceded his own work.

3. He refers to Paulus Fagius (1504–49), a professor of Hebrew first at Strasbourg and later at Cambridge. He describes his edition of *Pirke Avot* published in Isny in 1541 as the first Christian attempt to translate rabbinic literature. Wotton's privileging of this work as the first of this new scholarly tradition might have had something to do with Fagius' interest in demonstrating how Jewish sources could illuminate early Christian belief and practice. On him, see Richard Raubenheimer, *Paul Fagius aus Rheinzabern, sein Leben und Wirken als Reformator und Gelehrter* (Grünstadt, 1957); Jerome Friedman, *The Most Ancient Testimony: Sixteenth-Century Christian Hebraica in the Age of Renaissance Nostalgia* (Athens, Ohio, 1983), pp. 99–118; Piet van Boxel, "Waarom een christelijke hebraïst verbrand werd," *Ter Herkenning* 24 (1996): 107–19.

4. Johannes Cocceius (1603–69), a professor of theology at Leiden, was referred to by Wotton on more than one occasion. His edition of the Mishnah was

published in Amsterdam in 1629. On him, see van Asselt, *The Federal Theology of Johannes Cocceius (1603–1669)*; Yoffie, "Cocceius and the Jewish Commentators," 383–98; Aaron Katchen, *Christian Hebraists and Dutch Rabbis: Seventeenth-Century Apologetics and the Study of Maimonides'* Mishneh Torah (Cambridge, Mass., 1984), pp. 65–74; and William J. van Asselt, "Cocceius, Johannes," in Wiep van Bunge et al., eds., *Dictionary of Seventeenth- and Eighteenth-Century Dutch Philosophers*, 2 vols. (Bristol, England, 2003), 1:216–19.

5. On Constantijn L'Empereur (1591–1648), see Van Rooden, *Theology, Biblical Scholarship and Rabbinical Studies.* Van Rooden well contextualizes L'Empereur's works in relation to those of Fagius and Cocceius, pp. 100–132. The *Halichot Olam* mentioned by Wotton is the Hebrew title of *L'Empereur's Clavis Talmudica, complectens formulas, loca dialectica et rhetorica priscorum Judaeorum* (Leiden, 1634, 1714), his introduction to the Talmud. It surveys the content of the entire Talmud, explains rabbinic formulas and methods of interpreting the Bible, and summarizes how discussions in the Talmud are resolved. See also Katchen, *Christian Hebraists and Dutch Rabbis,* pp. 75–94.

6. On Sheringham and his *Joma Codex Talmudicus* (London, 1648), see Alastair Hamilton, "Sheringham, Robert (c. 1604–78)," *Oxford Dictionary of National Biography,* http://www.oxforddnb.com/view/article/25375. In the preface to his edition, Sheringham stresses the debt of the Gospels to Judaism, which can best be discovered by studying the *Talmud.* Sheringham was deeply committed to the royalist cause. After refusing to submit to Parliament, Sheringham forfeited his fellowship at Caius and departed for the Netherlands by 1651.

7. Wotton adds in a note: "To the Seder Zeraim or first Order of the Misna. To the Perek Chelek, i.e. the tenth Chapter of the Title Sanhedrin. To the Pirke Avoth. To the Seder Kodashim, or Order of consecrated Things. To the Seder Tahoroth, or Order of Purifications. To the Title Menacoth; or of Meat Offerings."

8. *Porta Mosis* (Oxford, 1655), translations of sections from Maimonides' *Mishneh Torah,* was an important contribution to the field. Pococke's work as a Hebraist and Arabist is nicely summarized by Gerald J. Toomer, "Pococke, Edward (1604–91)," *Oxford Dictionary of National Biography,* http://www.oxforddnb. com/view.article/22430, with recent bibliography. On his interest in Maimonides, see S. Levy, "English Students of Maimonides," *Jewish Historical Society of England Miscellanies* 4 (1942): 67–68.

9. Feingold, "Oriental Studies," in Nicholas Tyacke, ed., *Seventeenth-Century Oxford,* (Oxford, 1997), pp. 449–503, especially 465; Toomer, *Eastern Wisedome and Learning,* p. 293; and Alastair Hamilton, "Guise, William (Bap. 1652–d. 1683)," *Oxford Dictionary of National Biography,* http://www.oxforddnb.com/view/article/1729.

10. Johann Christoph Wagenseil (1633–1705) published his edition of Sotah in Altdorf in 1675, six years before his famous anthology *Tela ignea Satanae* appeared. For recent evaluations of the man and his work, see Harmut Bobzin, "Judenfeind oder Judenfreund? Die Altdorfer Gelehrte Johann Christoph Wagenseil," in *Jüdisches Leben in Franken,* ed. Gunnar Och and Hartmut Bobzin (Würzburg, 2002), pp. 33–51; and Peter Blastenbrei, *Johann Christoph Wagenseil und seine Stellung zum Judentum* (Erlangen, 2004).

11. He refers to Sebastian Schmid (1617–96), a professor of theology at Strasbourg, who first published in Latin *Mishnayot Masehktot Shabbat, hoc est Constiutiones tractatus Talmudici dicti Schabbath, cum commentarii celeberrimorum inter Judaeos magnique nominis rabbinorum Moses fil. Majemonis Aegypi et Obadjae de Bartenora* (Leipzig, 1661), and later *Collectaneorum Talmudicorum libri due, quorum prior*

de Sabbatho, posterior de Commixtis, Mishnas et Commentarios ad illas præscipuorum Rabbinorum cum versione Latina exhibet (Leipzig, 1670), in 2 parts. The volumes, printed in Hebrew and Latin, include a prefatory letter by Johann Benedict Carpzov, the younger, who was a professor of theology at Leipzig. On Schmid, see Jacob I. Dienstag, "Christian Translators of Maimonides' *Mishneh Torah* into Latin: A Bio-Bibliographical Survey," in Saul Lieberman and Arthur Hyman, eds., *Salo Wittmayer Baron Jubilee Volume,* 4 vols. (Jerusalem, 1974), English section, 1:301–2.

12. Hendrick Houting, *Massekhet Rosh-ha-Shanah sue tractatus talmudicus de festo novi anni* (Amsterdam, 1695), translated into Latin with annotation, and with the addition of his translation of the *Mishneh Torah,* Hilkhot Sanhedrin. See also *Encyclopedia Judaica* (Jerusalem, 1971), 8:37; Dienstag, "Christian Translators," p. 297; Daniel Lundius (1665–1747), *Massekhet Ta'anit, id et codex talmudicus de jejunio, ex Hebraeo sermone in Latinum verus, commentariisque illustratus a D. Lundio* (Trajecti ad Rhenum, 1694), in Hebrew and Latin.

13. John Selden (1584–1654) composed massive studies of the Noachide laws, marriage law, the Sanhedrin, the laws of tithes, and more. For a good summary with up-to-date bibliography, see Paul Christianson, "Selden, John (1584–1654)," *Oxford Dictionary of National Biography,* http://www.oxforddnb.com/view/article/25052; and especially Rosenblatt, *Renaissance England's Chief Rabbi.* Wotton adds in a note the titles of his books *History of Tithes. Uxor Ebraica. De successione in Pontificatum. De successionibus in bona Defuncti. De Anno Civili Veterum Judaeorum. De jure Naturali & Gentium secundum Disciplinam Ebraeorum. De Synedriis.*

14. John Lightfoot (1602–74) pioneered the use of rabbinic sources to elucidate the text and context of the New Testament, especially in his *Horae Hebraicae et Talmudicae* (Cambridge and London, 1658, 1663, 1671, 1674). For a good summary and recent bibliography, see Newton E. Key, "Lightfoot, John (1602–1675)," *Oxford Dictionary of National Biography,* http://www.oxforddnb.com/view/article/16648. Note Wotton's need to sing the praises of Selden, Lightfoot, and Pococke in this discussion of Mishnah editions despite the fact that none of them actually puts out an edition. But given their primary status in the history of Christian Hebraism in England, that is, as Wotton's immediate predecessors, he acknowledges their status in the field.

15. As I have indicated earlier, Surenhusius and his work are rightfully placed at the end of this progression, culminating in the complete edition and translation of the Mishnah.

16. On the many printed editions of the *Mishneh Torah* [= *Yad ha-Ḥazakah*], see Jacob I. [= Israel Jacob] Dienstag, "The *Mishneh Torah* of Maimonides: A Bibliography of Editions (Hebrew)," in Charles Berlin, ed., *Studies in Jewish Bibliography, History, and Literature in Honor of I. Edward Kiev* (New York, 1971), pp. 21–108.

17. Petrus Cunaeus (1586–1638) first published his *De Republica Hebraeorum* in Leiden in 1617 (English translation, London, 1653). He was the first non-Jew to make extensive use of the *Mishneh Torah* in his study of Jewish antiquities. See Katchen, *Christian Hebraists and Dutch Rabbis,* pp. 37–55; Jonathan Ziskind, "Petrus Cunaeus on Theocracy, Jubilee, and the Latifundia," *Jewish Quarterly Review* 68 (1978): 235–54; and Henri Krop, "Cunaeus Petrus," in *Dictionary of Seventeenth- and Eighteenth-Century Dutch Philosophers* (Bristol, 2003), 1:239–41.

18. On Joseph Scaliger (1540–1609) and his attitude toward Maimonides, see Katchen, *Christian Hebraists and Dutch Rabbis,* pp. 34–35; and generally, Grafton, *Joseph Scaliger: A Study in the History of Classical Scholarship;* and Wiep van Bunge, "Scaliger, Joseph," in *Dictionary of Seventeenth- and Eighteenth-Century Dutch Philosophers* 2:881–84. Louis (= Lodewijk) De Dieu (1590–1642) composed *Critica sacra*

sive animadversions in loca quaedam difficiliora Veteris et Novi Testamenti (Amsterdam, 1693). On Thomas Erpenius (1584–1624), see Van Rooden, *Theology, Biblical Scholarship, and Rabbinical Studies,* pp. 57–64; and Theo Verbeek, "Erpenius, Thomas," in *Dictionary of Seventeenth- and Eighteenth-Century Dutch Philosophers* 1:338–39. Erpenius, who was primarily an Arabist, was appointed a professor of Oriental languages in Leiden in 1613, excluding Hebrew, and of Hebrew in 1619. He published several introductory Hebrew works, including a famous oration on the Hebrew and Arabic languages, *Orationes tres de Linguarum Ebreae et Arabicae Dignitate* (Leiden, 1621). He also was the teacher of L'Empereur. Jakob Golius (1596–1667) was also Erpenius's student and became a professor of Arabic studies at Leiden. See J. Brugman, "Arabic Scholarship," in Th. H. Lunsingh Scheurleer and G. H. M. Posthumus Meyjes, eds., *Leiden University in the Seventeenth Century: An Exchange of Learning,* (Leiden, 1975), pp. 202–15; and J. Brugman and F. Schröder, *Arabic Studies in the Netherlands* (Leiden, 1979); Wilhelmina M. C. Juynboll, *Zeventiende-eeuwsche beoefenaars van het arabisch in Nederland* (Utrecht, 1931).

19. Dionysius Vossius (1612–42), the son of Gerard Johannes, was L'Empereur's student in Leiden. Menasseh ben Israel also instructed him, for which Vossius repaid him by translating several of his works into Latin. In 1636 he completed his translation of the laws of idolatry in the *Mishneh Torah.* It was published posthumously as *R. Moses Maimonidae De Idolatria Liber* (Amsterdam, 1642). The work reveals the author's vast knowledge of classical and pagan sources, although his Hebraic references are more modest. On him, see Van Rooden, *Theology, Biblical Scholarship, and Rabbinical Studies,* pp. 190–92; Dienstag, "Christian Translators," pp. 305–6; C. S. M. Rademaker, *The Life and Work of Gerardus Joannes Vossius 1577–1649* (Assen, 1981); and especially, Katchen, *Christian Hebraists and Dutch Rabbis,* pp. 161–235.

20. Georgius Gentius (1618–87) was also a student of Menasseh ben Israel. He translated Maimonides' *Hilkhot De'ot* into Latin as *Meimonidis Canones ethici* (Amsterdam, 1640) and also completed Menasseh's translation of Solomon Ibn Verga's *Shevet Yehudah,* published as *Historia Judaica* (Amsterdam, 1651). See Katchen, *Christian Hebraists and Dutch Rabbis,* pp. 247–68; Van Rooden, *Theology, Biblical Scholarship, and Rabbinical Studies,* pp. 193–94; and Dienstag, "Christian Translators," pp. 294–95.

21. Guglielmus [= Johannes] Vorstius (d. 1652) was both a pupil of Menasseh ben Israel and the translator of one of his works. He was also a student of L'Empereur. He translated Maimonides's *Hilkhot Yesodei ha-Torah* as *Constitutiones de fundamentis legis,* with the Hebrew text and commentary of Abravanel, in Amsterdam in 1638. He also translated Abravanel's *Rosh Amanah,* David Gans's *Zemah David,* and the *Pirke de R. Eliezer.* See Katchen, *Christian Hebraists and Dutch Rabbis,* pp. 235–47; Van Rooden, *Theology, Biblical Scholarship, and Rabbinical Studies,* pp. 173–74, 191–92; and Dienstag, "Christian Translators," pp. 304–5. Wotton's criticisms of Vorstius's translations might be attributed to the fact that he was the son of the heterodox theologian Conradus Vorstius and displayed throughout his work a hostile criticism of Jews and Judaism.

22. Prideaux published his Latin translation and commentary of a section of Maimonides's law code entitled *De jure pauperis et peregrini* in London in 1679. On Prideaux, see especially Chapter 1 above as well as de Quehen's essay, "Prideaux, Humphrey," in the *Oxford Dictionary of National Biography,* http://www.oxforddnb.com/view/article/22784; Holt, "The Treatment of Arab History by Prideaux, Ockley, and Sale," pp. 290–302; Dienstag, "Christian Translators,"

pp. 299–300; Levy, "English Students," pp. 68–69; and Bernardini, "The Silent Retreat of the Fathers," pp. 102–8.

23. Robert Clavering (1675/6–1747), a Hebraist and the bishop of Peterborough, published his bilingual editions of two tracts of Maimonides, *Hilkhot Talmud Torah* and *Teshuvah*, as *R. Mosis Maimonidis tractatus due* (Oxford, 1705), with extensive annotation and a profile of Maimonides. On Clavering, see Scott Mandelbrote, "Clavering, Robert (1675/6–1747)," *Oxford Dictionary of National Biography,* http://www.oxforddnb.com/view/article/5554; Dienstag, "Christian Translators," p. 291; and Levy, "English Students," p. 74.

24. Note that Wotton's primary interest was in legal discussions, not simply moral or cultural matters. It underscores both his primary concern that understanding the legal system of the Jews would lead to a clearer understanding of the New Testament and his own self-image of what his chief contribution was to this discipline.

25. Wotton refers, with obvious personal knowledge and appreciation, to Lewis Compiégne de Veil (1637–?), who converted to the Catholic Church with his brother in 1665. Under Colbert, he published in 1667 in Paris *Ex Rabbi Mosis Majemonidae opera quod manus forti inscribitur, Tractatus tre: 1. De Ieiunio. 2. De solemnitat expiationun. 3. De solemnitate Paschatis*; in 1669 in Paris *Ex Mosis Majemonidae opera, quod secunda lex., sive manus fortis, inscribitur, Tractatus de Consecratione Calendarum, & de Ratione intercalendi*; in Paris in 1673 *Hebraeorum de connubiis jus civile et Pontificium: Seu Ex R. Moses . . . eo libro, qui est de uxoria, tractatus primus*; and in Paris in 1678 *De cultu divino, ex Mosis Majemonidae secunda lege seu manu forti liber VIII . . . in quibus exprimitur Hierosolymitani Templi forma.* In 1696 these same translations were republished in a larger edition. After becoming a Protestant and immigrating to England, under the patronage of Viscount Hyde, he continued to publish his translations. He republished in London in 1683 *R. Moses Majemonidae de Sacrificiis liber . . . et Majemonidae Tractaus de Consecratione Calendarum et de ratione intercalandi*; and in Paris in 1688 *De culto divino liber, tractatus novem continens.* He also translated Abraham Yagel's Hebrew catechism into Latin in London in 1679. On du Veil, see Levy "English Students," pp. 71–74; and Dienstag, "Christian Translators," pp. 303–4. Wotton adds a source for his remark in a note: "Dedit nobis eadem Anglis Proemium Commentariorum Abarbinelis in Leviticum, quod Latinum fecit Ludovicus Compeigne de Veil, qui multos Tractatus e Maimonidis Pandectis Judaicis Latio dedit; & si puritatem Latini Sermonis spectemus, omnibus Interpretibus palmam praeripuit. *Relandi Prolegomen. In Analect. Rabbin.*" The reference is to Adriaan Reelant (1676–1718), *Analecta Rabbinica, comprehendentia libellos quosdam singulars et alia quae ad lectionem . . . Commentariorum Rabbinicorum faciunt* (Utrecht, 1792).

26. He refers to *R. Mosis Maimonidis Tractatus de vacca rufa Latinitate donatus & subjuncta ampliore husjus ritus explicatione quoad singulas circumstantias illustratus ab Andrea Christophoro Zellero* (Amsterdam, 1711, 1713). On Zeller (1684–1743), see *Encyclopedia Judaica,* 8:67; Dienstag, "Christian Translators," p. 307.

27. It is obvious that Wotton, despite his great admiration for Maimonides' work, recognized the limitations of the *Mishneh Torah* as an authoritative code of law. He perhaps exaggerates its insignificance by deeming it merely the opinions of an interpreter, like Rashi or Bertinora, who is in no position to challenge the legal rulings of the *Mishnah* and the *Gemarah,* which Wotton sees as the ultimate authority in determining Jewish normative behavior. Wotton does not address in this discussion the other codes of Jewish law: the *Turim* and the *Shulkhan Arukh* and their less ambiguous status as authoritative law codes. His preference to

consider the Mishnah as the purest and ultimate expression of Jewish law, even for contemporary Jews, surely prevents him from seeing the Jewish legal tradition as an ever expanding and living organism rather than one fixed in time and never changing and evolving. Not only is his view naïve, but it seems necessary for him given the degree to which he was invested in elucidating the Mishnah alone as the primary Jewish source for elucidating ancient Christianity. For a succinct discussion of the status of the *Mishneh Torah* as a law code, see Isadore Twersky, *Introduction to the Code of Maimonides (Mishneh Torah)* (New Haven, Conn., 1980), pp. 515–37.

28. He refers to the Roman Catholic theologian Thomas Stapleton (1535–98), Cardinal Roberto Bellarmino (1542–1621), and Cardinal Jacques Davy Du Perron (1556–1618), all important leaders of the Catholic reform movement of the sixteenth century. Notwithstanding their considerable authority in enforcing Church law and discipline, Wotton maintains, they still functioned as individuals who interpreted the law, not as ultimate decisors in their own right. What is interesting about this remark is Wotton's inclination to find favorable comparisons between the Catholic and Jewish legal traditions, viewing both, it appears, as resting on law, in contrast to his own Protestant one. And he is equally consistent in seeing neither a rabbinic law code nor the catechism of a church council as having binding legal power on either religious community.

Index

Acknowledgments

The idea of this book emerged in the inspiring ambiance of the reading rooms of the new British Library in London. I am most indebted to the staff of this scholarly paradise as well as the staff of my own institutional library of the University of Pennsylvania, especially that of its unique Center for Advanced Judaic Studies.

I relied heavily on several generous colleagues and friends who offered to read earlier versions of this narrative and provide me with invaluable critical comments. I want to thank especially Arthur Kiron, Justin Champion, Todd Endelman, Matt Goldish, David Katz, Jason Rosenblatt, Andrea Schatz, Adam Shear, and Elisheva Carlebach. I wrestled with all of their comments and suggestions and accepted many of them. I am especially indebted to my editor and colleague Jerome Singerman of the University of Pennsylvania Press, who not only welcomed my manuscript but read it carefully and offered wise counsel in restructuring its argument. I am also grateful to Erica Ginsburg and Christine Sweeney for their editorial assistance.

I had the privilege of speaking about this project before several exciting audiences at the University of Düsseldorf, the Free University of Berlin, Ohio State University, and the Clark Library at the University of California, Los Angeles. I want to thank all the colleagues I met at these occasions for their stimulating observations and suggestions.

I am grateful to the history department of the University of Pennsylvania for allowing me time away from my usual duties to work on this project. I am most appreciative of my wonderful staff at the Center for Advanced Judaic Studies for taking on additional burdens during my absence as director. Sheila Allen, Sam Cardillo, Natalie Dohrmann, and Elsie Stern deserve special thanks. Judith Leifer and Etty Lassman were helpful to me in researching and preparing this manuscript for press. My wife, Phyllis, understood my need to work on this project during two sabbaticals and as usual gave me her full support and love. As always, I am enormously indebted to her.